PRINCIPAL'S GUIDELINES FOR
ACTION IN PARENT CONFERENCES

PRINCIPAL'S GUIDELINES FOR ACTION IN PARENT CONFERENCES

JAMES N. CASAVIS

PARKER PUBLISHING COMPANY, INC.

West Nyack, N.Y.

LIBRARY OF CONGRESS
CATALOG CARD NUMBER: 72–121710

PRINTED IN THE UNITED STATES OF AMERICA
ISBN-0-13-702001-5
B&P

About This Book and

Today's Parent Conferences . . .

The need to write this book grew out of a compulsion to better understand the parent-teacher relationship.

As an elementary school principal, I began to develop an awareness of the complexities of the contemporary school. I sought an approach to parent-teacher conferences which would prove helpful to the hard-pressed and oftentimes confused school teachers and administrators caught in a period of rapid change.

The case studies in this book are the result of years of careful note taking. All cases reported are composites of many different parent-conference situations. Names of parents, teachers, students and situations have all been changed and each case has been given a number–letter designation such as case 501S so that any similarity in name or place is coincidental.

The author, in attempting to sharply focus the readers' sights on emerging middle-class suburban patterns, has stereotyped a community setting in the expectation that more vivid images will be presented.

Chapter One states that the mother "rearranges her time with a precision that would be the envy of a production manager." The father, "as he releases more and more of his family commitments to his wife, withdraws and becomes a less active participant in family decisions."

There are upper middle-class suburban mothers who are not efficient household managers and fathers in middle-class suburbia who run a patriarchal home, but the emerging patterns in suburbia more and more indicate control of the home in the hands of the mother.

The visible changes that are occurring in American society today with its parent sit-ins and speak-outs are not limited to the suburbs. It is not an accident that some superintendents, board members and teachers leave town after community pressure is applied.

As an involved schoolman, I am reacting to and working within a suburban, metropolitan area, near a large city. The approaches developed in this book are becoming more familiar nationwide as the affluent, metropolitan, contemporary culture spreads. The involved schoolman and interested parent will find this book especially relevant.

J. N. C.

ACKNOWLEDGMENTS

I am indebted to the many teachers, administrators and children who have given me insights into everyday school relationships.

I am most appreciative of my real teachers, the parents, who have, in attempting to make me aware of their dissatisfaction, helped me better to understand the contemporary scene.

I am especially appreciative of suggestions and guidance from the following school professionals:

Mrs. Ronald Bayles, Mr. Orlando Canale, Mrs. Marvin Gess, Mr. Paul Kissel, Mrs. Martin Lindenberg, Mrs. James Lynch, Dr. Ralph McMillen, Mrs. Seymour Spatz and Mr. Nicholas Zeverino.

Contents

PRINCIPAL'S GUIDELINES FOR
ACTION IN PARENT CONFERENCES

A Contemporary View

of the Parent-Teacher Relationship

The setting of this book while not unique is one where many of today's social and economic pressures are etched on the public schools.

Consider a rapid-growth suburban community within earshot of New York City. The sounds from the city are of racial unrest, overcrowdedness, inadequate schools and the upward mobility of the middle class.

Observe the large potato farms as they give way to the burgeoning housing developments. Listen to the dissident sounds of the city as they strike the ears of the now affluent middle class. A mass exodus of panic proportions ensues.

The Family

The contemporary metropolitan family in seeking a suburban home gravitates toward a housing development which has similar social and economic levels. Similarities in age, husbands' salaries, educational background and religious affiliation are commonplace. The parents of the young couple often make the down payment on the house. Furniture and extras—such as central air-conditioning, a fireplace and a swimming pool—are given as gifts by the grandparents so that the grandchildren "may live in the country."

15

Our nuclear-age family soon finds that local taxes rise sharply. A second car is needed and the demands of temple dues, church pledges, and keeping the best foot forward place a severe crimp on the family budget. The revolving credit-card game helps to continue the flow of goods and services while adding to the anxieties of the new way of life.

The joys of leaving the crowded city are tempered by finding that many of the well-known services and facilities once taken for granted are no longer available.

The new arrivals find that perhaps unlike the city the suburb encourages them to participate in town and school activities. They are urged to speak out on community and school issues and to help formulate plans for change.

The newcomers demand sewerage, increased school facilities, better roads and more sidewalks.

The civic association becomes the focal point in fighting for local improvement. The association becomes the nesting ground for young, ambitious lawyers who aspire to get ahead. This pressure group in making demands on the established community, creates friction and brings about change. The association gets its own members on the board of education and begins to make inroads into the established fraternal clubs and political parties.

The mother begins to redo her nest. She rearranges her time with a precision that would be the envy of a production manager. Cleaning women are secured, the children's after-school activities are arranged, social commitments to bowling teams, card games and informal coffee klatches are set. Temple and church dates are all cleared on an ever-crowded calendar. The manipulation of monies is effected through the husband's salary, bank loans, credit-card rotation and the ever-present grandparents. Long weekend trips to the hotel resorts and to the Caribbean are managed. Hair and clothes styles are priorities in a way of life where staying young and attractive are musts.

The father, now a commuter, finds that his working day has increased due to travel time. He leaves the house earlier and returns later. The increased cost of living in the suburbs has placed an additional burden on his shoulders. As he releases more and more of his family commitments to his wife, he withdraws and becomes a less active participant in family decisions.

The father who spends most of his time on the road creates additional family problems. The home becomes matrilineal. The traditional male role, so vital for the son's identification, must be learned elsewhere. The husband who travels to Los Angeles, Detroit and other places touches home base only on occasion. He is viewed by his children as a visitor and by his wife as a guest in the house. Recreational sex, a game played by many upper middle-class parents, further reshuffles adult values in an already fast-changing culture.

The Student's Viewpoint

The child, unlike his parents who were raised in an adult-centered society, finds himself in an affluent child-centered one. He is both a reflection of the family's present success and its future aspirations. He is highly motivated to achieve at school. His aggressions find an outlet in verbalism. He becomes highly skilled in relating to both teacher and parent. A degree of sophistication in maneuvering adults is developed. Institutionalization through nursery schools, after-school cultural activities and day camps further prepares him for the suburban way of life. The future is carefully planned for the child as he is walked through proper pre-mating contacts so that he may with ease find his place in the new society. As a parent said to me, "As long as my daughter is going to fall in love, she might as well fall in love with a rich man as a poor man; after all, this makes a lot of things easier."

The public school grows in leaps and bounds. The pressing need is for space, and the school administrators become mortar and brick men. The unusual emphasis placed upon success through education puts the school professional in the spotlight. The professional responds to these pressures by accommodating the public through an endless series of phone conversations, conferences and meetings to develop balances, compromises and "let's wait awhile" situations.

A decision that is made today may be undone tomorrow.

A number of parents, when told by the principal that no more money was available for playground equipment, formed an action committee and petitioned the superintendent. Later that afternoon the principal was notified by the business office that he should re-order the playground equipment.

A suburban local board of education told the superintendent that it would be necesary to develop more innovations in the elementary schools. "What about team teaching?" the board president asked. The superintendent said that this sounded good and that he would look into it. Later in the week, the superintendent presented a plan to the board and they approved it. The next day the superintendent called the principal and told him that he would have a team teaching program. The principal, having lived through many an innovation, replied, "That's nice."

Inefficiency in the schools is not unknown and even when well organized, the energy expended playing the suburban game of schoolmanship soon exhausts the educator. As a result much of his time and energy is expended on a chess game which usually ends in a stalemate. Some schoolmen remain relatively unaffected owing to a lack of understanding of what is actually happening about them. Others develop an attitude of "well this is how you play the game."

The teacher, middle class oriented, either through family or college training, has many skills with parents. He readily "tunes in" as he works with parent and child. He has learned to accommodate and, like his administrator, he plays his role well. The contemporary teacher, unlike the teacher of a generation ago, sees his profession as only one part of his varied life.

As I worked within this framework, I began to realize that an approach as unique as is the current setting was needed by teachers in solving parent concerns. The time-honored attempts at parent-teacher conferences would not work, for pouring new wine into old bottles was not the answer.

At this point I became aware of the nonconfrontational method.

CHAPTER TWO

Four Approaches

to the Parent Conference

The opportunity to study teachers working with parents in upper middle-class suburban settings enabled me to put to the test some of my ideas about the parent conference.

My own insights and experiences with the middle-class parent told me that the nonconfrontational approach worked. Although I had gathered data on different conference techniques I never seriously questioned why some approaches worked in some situations and not in others.

I was able to identify four approaches to parent conferences that staff members used: (1) nonconfrontational, (2) confrontational, (3) indirect, and (4) direct.

The Nonconfrontational Approach

1. Hostility is dissipated
2. Shared concerns
3. Accepting nonthreatening atmosphere
4. Structuring of the problem
5. Follow-up meeting

As the four approaches to parent conferences are described, the terms "teacher" and "teacher-counselor" are used interchangeably because the author views each teacher as a teacher-counselor when working with parents.

The nonconfrontational method implies an indirect approach. It implies a friendly, accepting atmosphere where initial hostility is dissipated and where a head-on conflict is avoided.

The bearing and the composure of the teacher set the stage. He approaches the parent in a relaxed manner, always keeping in mind that he is in control of the situation. He gauges his speech and his attitude so that the parent does not feel that the teacher is an intruder.

The teacher should not have a parent conference when he is tense and troubled if at all possible. Anxiety on the part of the teacher may distort his objectivity and cause him to read his own concerns into the conference.

A difficult day with the children may be just cause for the teacher to call off an after-school parent conference. The harm that may result from a negative parent-teacher conference will far outweigh the inconvenience to the parent in changing his appointment.

The parent generally initiates the meeting by posing the problem. The parent usually has a definite concern, be it real or imaginary. He has a list of grievances and possibly some solutions to his problem.

It is not unusual to have a parent come to a conference armed to prove a point. Some parents "come on very strong" and are abusive.

The middle-class parent often phones other parents in order to fortify his position so that when he confronts the teacher he attacks him on a number of fronts.

A teacher may be abusively berated in an initial onslaught that tests his mettle. This is all the more reason for the teacher to be relaxed and confident of his own position.

The solutions offered by the parent are usually reflections of the parent's background and especially of his own school experiences.

The teacher should be aware that we are living at a time in history where all authority is being challenged and the teacher is viewed by parents as a symbol of that authority. The teacher represents the establishment and he should be aware that anti-establishment feelings are found not only in politics, religion and government but also in the schools.

This prime concern period is necessary for the release of feelings. At this point the teacher attempts to evaluate the total situation and to reform a working structure of the problem. Feeling tones, facts, biases and possible solutions may all be presented that can help in the final resolution of the problem. The teacher listens carefully and recaps the real and the imaginary circumstances. This informational session avoids any immediate decision or direct replies which could retard the initial flow of concerns. Erroneous information is corrected and factual presentations are made at this point. The sensitivity of the teacher aids in setting the pace and the structure of the conference.

It is obvious at this point that the nonconfrontational teacher is a highly skilled, sensitive counselor of adults. The ability to listen with sensitivity to a parent who may be quite emotional and to separate the factual happenings from statements that are emotionally charged and wish-fulfilling requires a mature, experienced teacher-counselor.

It is clear that the teacher is thinking in terms of human relationships and has developed an empathy for parent problems.

When the problem is presented in the form of a threat, the teacher does well to listen attentively and to try to pick out a thread of information that will bring about some grounds for a minor agreement to be built upon. For no reason does the teacher show tension and anxiety. It is important for the parent to feel that the teacher is interested and that time permits the problem to be aired. The teacher does not interrupt or interject his thoughts during this preliminary period.

The assumption here is that the parent is so upset that a ventilation of his concerns is needed.

This attempt to find some area of agreement helps to establish something, however minor, to agree on. This dissipates some hostility and may lessen the fears of the anxious, insecure parent who "comes on strong" to cover up his own inadequacies.

The time factor is an important one and the teacher may want to schedule the conference after school. It is better for the teacher to plan the time so that he may go home rather than back to the class if the conference appears to be a difficult one.

As free a flow of communication is permitted as possible. Oftentimes talking around the question by the teacher is wise because a direct answer may accentuate concerns and anxieties. The acknowledgment of insights and shared concerns on the part of the teacher paves the way for further agreements. An outburst of hostility may be all that is needed. It is possible that this discussion may satisfy the parent. He may feel that now somebody really cares and having been listened to or having told somebody off, the need for satisfaction has been taken care of.

Here again, the sensitive teacher-counselor gauges the intensity of the parent concern.

There are some parent conferences where the teacher realizes after an initial concern period on the part of the parent that some information or reassurance is all that is needed.

The teacher-counselor also differentiates between the chronic complainer and the parent with a genuine concern. Fortunately the chronic complainer is in the minority.

The societal class pressures of upward mobility imposed upon the parent often bring about the need for a conference to reassure and reaffirm that everything is going alright.

Often a follow-up session is needed and in this way additional information may be gathered. This also allows for a cooling-off period.

The teacher who has been approached by a parent who states that this or that did or did not happen would do well to have a follow-up conference, rather than to commit himself to something that he is not sure of. The parent may very well have found out something that the teacher doesn't know about, and the teacher by setting a time for another conference gives himself an opportunity to become better acquainted with the total situation. The teacher in this way has another opportunity to gain insights into the child's behavior.

As the first conference period draws to a close, the teacher attempts to bring the session to a positive conclusion. The teacher summarizes some of the facts discussed. He allays some of the fears and the misconceptions presented. A follow-up meeting is set at this point.

The teacher uses his skills of accommodation when he brings a conference to a positive conclusion.

He may find that concessions have been made on each side and that although some issues have not been settled the overt conflict has been avoided.

These social expedients for reducing tensions permit people to cooperate more fully.

The accepting, nonthreatening atmosphere, the primary talk-through session, the presentation and structuring of the problem, and the follow-up meeting are all part of this nonconfrontational method.

The Confrontational Approach

1. A conflict situation is developed
2. A head-on struggle
3. A coolness in relationships

The confrontational method is one in which a conflict situation is developed either by the parent, the teacher-counselor or both. The person or persons who intiate this approach usually are so involved in an emotionally charged situation that a head-on struggle becomes inevitable.

The teacher or the parent who can hardly wait to tell the other person off illustrates this kind of situation. The meeting generally is affected by a coolness in relationships where either one or both parties approach the conference in a most formal, guarded fashion. Information, accusations and deep concerns are exchanged outside of an understanding framework. A shouting match or at best an exchange of accusations occurs.

I recall one conference that I participated in where after the teacher and the parent parried each other's efforts at reaching an understanding, a shouting match began:

Parent: "You are not qualified to teach school!"
Teacher: "You, sir, are making many assumptions!"
Parent: "My boy is wasting his time in your class!"
Teacher: "Your son is just plain immature!"
Parent: "I'm going to go straight to the superintendent!"
Teacher: "Go ahead!"

There are some educators who believe that there are times when a confrontation should be consciously developed in order to shake a parent who is adamant about an obvious situation. By unhinging the parent, it is hoped that one may restructure the situation on a more realistic basis.

Although I don't accept this kind of "parent shock treatment," I can see times when a parent has to be shaken out of his lethargy.

I recall one vivid case conference where the principal of a junior high school in an affluent suburban area counseled the mother of a precocious seventh-grade girl. The mother felt threatened by her daughter. It appeared that the girl was winning the father's attention to the point where the mother was ignored by the father. He was totally unaware of what was happening and it was necessary for the principal to sit down and confront him with the situation. The father became very abusive and threatened to go to the board of education and have the principal reprimanded.

At this point the principal brought in the mother and after a tumultuous session the father accepted the fact that his daughter was purposely creating situations that would place her mother in an unfavorable light.

The teacher would do well when he perceives a difficult conference ahead to gather as much information as possible about the current situation. Permanent record cards, record folders, information on previous conferences, and comments from other teachers who know the parent should be evaluated.

The principal may be requested to sit in on the meeting. A third person who is responsible for the total program can often provide an important balance wheel and inject a more objective note into the conference.

The third man concept is not unknown in education. Actually this type of arbitration, the utilization of a third party either to settle a dispute or to help interpret what is being said, is important when an impasse is reached between the teacher and the parent. In these cases the principal uses his office to develop an objective understanding of the current case and he also may call upon other resource professionals at his disposal.

Unfortunately there are times when a parent will view the inclusion of a psychologist, a guidance counselor or a social worker as another way that the school has of putting the parent down.

The teacher in consultation with the principal may use a team approach and ask the psychologist, the social worker or the nurse to be part of the conference before a confrontation develops with the parent.

There may be times when it is better to put off the conference and in this way provide for a cooling-off period. I have known teachers who have conveniently cancelled these kinds of conferences to good advantage. At other times it is best to hear the parent out.

As in all parent conferences, the sensitivity of the teacher-counselor and the timing of the meeting are crucial factors that help determine the success or the failure of the conference.

The confrontational conference is the most difficult of meetings for both the parent and the teacher to work through. Yet this method is sometimes inevitable, and when this is the case, a more formal structure may be used by the teacher calling in supportive personnel. It may take a longer period of time to resolve the problem.

In a later chapter I present one case that not only reached an unsatisfactory conclusion but to my knowledge, to this day, is still unresolved.

The Indirect Approach

1. The teacher acts as a sounding board for the parent's concerns
2. Cathartic-type conferences
3. A verbal discharge

The indirect method utilized in the parent conference is one where the teacher acts as a sounding board for the parent's concerns. The teacher-counselor listens while the parent talks. The teacher may simply be a good listener and lend a sympathetic ear. He may by facial expressions show his empathy for the parent. He may encourage the parent to tell him more about the concern by occasionally injecting an encouraging word or by suggesting a lead question.

The parent finds this approach one where he can get off his chest things that not only bother him about this situation but also about other unrelated situations.

Parent: "Jimmy often runs to his room with his hands over his ears so that he cannot hear Mr. Z and me argue."

"Jimmy says that he is afraid of you. Can't you find time in class to praise him?"

Teacher: "Oh?"

Parent: "Well, maybe Jimmy is not really afraid of you, with all that is going on at home, well maybe he is caught up in it."

The teacher finds this kind of verbal discharge enervating and while the parent transfers his concerns to the teacher, the teacher in turn may develop a degree of anxiety himself.

A very emotionally charged parent monologue frees the parent of concerns and guilt while it leaves the teacher with an exhaustion that will be with him for the rest of the day.

I have had teachers that have left these cathartic-type conferences in need of several aspirin.

Teachers would do well to schedule these tiring conferences for the end of the day. They are both exhausting and time-consuming.

A teacher who uses this approach may encourage the parent to come back for another session and the teacher may walk the parent through a number of these conferences before he approaches the concerns that the child has in the room.

One obvious danger, of course, is that the parent becomes so dependent upon these talk-throughs that they are continued for a very long period of time. The teacher should set definite limitations as the parent begins to approach an understanding of his child's concerns.

I have known parents who have called teachers every night just to be reassured.

There is also the obvious danger that the teacher may become involved in playing the role of a psychologist or a family counselor.

I caution teachers that when it is evident that psychological or family guidance is needed, they should refer the parent to the proper agency.

Some teachers are highly successful with this method and use it in preference to other approaches. I suspect that certain teachers—those who tend to listen, who are less verbal, and who are unaggressive—do well with this approach.

I have found that skilled teacher-counselors use different approaches at different times and are able to sense when an indirect approach is needed.

I have observed some parents who seek out this kind of conference. The age and the sex of the teacher are not as important as in the case of the direct method.

This may have implications for the young female teacher who often is seen as a competitor by the mature mother. This young-woman–mature-mother competition is further emphasized by a culture that puts an emphasis on being young.

It is a well-known fact in suburbia, that the young male, beginning teacher does not have the same parent pressures as the young female, beginning teacher.

The Direct Approach

1. Telling, imparting one
2. Highly structured
3. The parent is a passive member of the conference

The direct approach is the one that has most frequently been used by teachers. This method assumes that the teacher is the authority figure who has something worthwile to tell the parent. It also assumes that the parent looks to the teacher for guidance and information.

It is obvious that in an upper middle-class community this is not often the case. Many parents have more education than the teachers. Status parents, having a high standing in the community, are not usually receptive to advice from a teacher who not only may be viewed as on a lower rung of the social ladder but who may be considerably younger than the parent.

Age and sex are important factors in using the direct approach. A young unmarried woman teacher may be viewed by a mature mother as one who has not had enough life experiences to talk with authority about her child.

One exasperated mother while complaining about her child's teacher stated, "My daughter has a brand-new teacher right out of college. I'm really doubtful that a twenty-one-year-old girl knows how to handle a class. Again, I don't like to criticize anyone who is so young, but I doubt that a person this young has much patience."

The direct approach is a telling, imparting one. It is generally highly structured and often it is supported by test marks, class papers, classroom observations and educational statements. Generally little room is left for parents to air concerns.

A teacher in working with a parent stated, "Bill is not working anywhere near his potential. He does very little in school. He does not get along well with the other children in his class."

The direct approach uses a number of time-honored techniques. Some take-home material such as test scores, especially the machine-scored ones, are used.

The conference generally begins on a positive note with interesting, informative visual aids that pinpoint the student's progress. The teacher paces himself after he has made his major points and then summarizes the conference. The teacher leaves the door open for further meetings.

This direct conference method is highly regarded by most teachers although teachers are becoming more and more aware that the conference is a relationship situation and that in some communities such as the suburban middle-class ones a more active involvement by the parent is needed.

Still the direct method has an appeal to many teachers because it is a telling approach and the one many use in working with children in the classroom.

The parent is substituted for the child in the teacher's mind. The teacher then views Mrs. J as a large edition of her daughter, Ruth. This is not difficult to do as physical and psychological characteristics are sometimes quite similar in a family.

It is not unusual to hear a teacher say that after meeting Mrs. J she now understands Ruth. "Why they even both have the same nervous twitch in the left eye," exclaimed a teacher.

When a teacher uses this kind of parent-child substitution, the role of the teacher remains basically unchanged and the security of the teacher is left unchallenged.

While this method does not generally work well when used by young teachers in an upper middle-class community it does have positive results when used by a mature, highly respected teacher. Here again the teacher's age, sex and experience are important factors in the success of this method.

The contemporary upper middle-class parent who learns well from a dialogue method may be participating more as a passive member of the conference and getting less from this approach. The need to be actively involved in a discussion and to act out feelings which characterizes the middle-class woman may largely negate some of the effectiveness of this approach.

This is not surprising as more and more the middle-class parent is becoming action-centered. He finds many satisfactions in direct participation. The need to talk through concerns and to be part of the process rather than a passive observer is found today in many areas of living. Witness the unrest in some churches and the changes that have been undertaken to have more lay people play an active role.

It is true that as people become involved in a situation in an active sense, they are more stimulated and they tend to participate more in the end results.

In the next four chapters I have isolated a number of actual case conferences. These conferences have been grouped, based on the conference approach used. An attempt has been made to present these cases and to analyze why certain approaches were used and the relative success or the failure of each approach.

CHAPTER THREE

Dialogues Showing

the Nonconfrontational Approach

The three case conferences that follow represent examples of the nonconfrontational approach. In each case, the parents are angry and they present their concerns in a direct way accusing either the teacher, the principal or the school board of irregularities. In any one of these cases, the principal could have caused a confrontational situation by using an approach similar to the parents'. Instead, the principal has attempted to reassure the parents by pointing out the positive aspects of their concerns and by structuring the discussion into less hostile channels.

It is important for the reader to study the approach that the principal uses which is found in all three dialogues because this approach does dissipate parent hostility and it prepares the way for a more reasonable discussion of the problems presented.

School complaints are often presented to the schoolman in a direct way and it is incumbent upon the school authorities to reassure the parent while at the same time reducing the initial anxiety to a level where common understandings may be arrived at.

The practical value to the schoolman is that the discussion does not get out of hand and is handled at the local school level. Far too many initial phone calls and parent conferences are not handled well and land in the lap of the superintendent. These in turn have to go back to the principal and be reworked again in a more effective manner.

A Request to Change Teachers

Case no. 501 S

Mrs. S: "My husband and I have come in to see you before school starts to ask that you change Joseph to another teacher. I'm sure that Mrs. B is very nice but I want a teacher for Joseph who is more than just a technician."

Mr. S: "That's right. I just flew in from my Detroit office when I heard that Joseph was not getting a superior teacher. He has had one mediocre teacher after another. I have a list here of teachers whom I don't want for my son."

Principal: "I'm glad that both of you came in today for I know that you have had some concerns over the past few years about the teachers. In checking the records I find that Joseph has had two teachers with over ten years of experience and two teachers with two years of experience. Mrs. B, his new teacher, has a master's degree and four years of teaching experience. I mention this as we all are aware that in a school district such as ours we lose many fine teachers to some of the better paying school systems near us. A student in our district is apt to have an inexperienced teacher at least once every three years. I believe that you will agree that Joseph has been able to have experienced teachers every year."

Mr. S: "I'm sure that we can do business. Look, I have people working for me and I make changes every day. All I'm asking is that Joseph be switched to a better teacher."

Mrs. S: "Yes, my husband is right. After all this is a special case. Joseph has been treated as a number since he has been in public school."

Principal: "Our school now is experiencing a very heavy influx from the city. Some classes have as many as thirty-eight students. Even so we are exploring many different ways to help children. For instance, with our new audio-visual materials we are able to reach children on a more personalized basis."

Mr. S: "This all my be true; however, I know that this may be my last chance to influence you. Once school opens you will not permit children to change classes."

Principal: "I'm glad that you mentioned room changes. Children will certainly be tested and changed to other rooms as they show the teachers that they are ready for more challenging work. Any room changes, of course, are carefully controlled by our testing program."

Mr. S: "You mention room changes based on a testing program. Why can't teachers strive for quality? It seems as though children are just given busy work. They don't have a chance to express themselves. Why, Joseph has not even been reached."

Principal: "I will speak to Mrs. B and we will set up a conference on September 26th. In this way we will know Joseph a little better. At that time I will present to you all available information that we have on Joseph. This will include test results, class work and any information that we have in his permanent record folder."

Mr. S: "You are forcing me to accept your point of view."

Principal: "We must figure out new ways to reach each other rather than the outworn methods that we have used in the past. I will have Mrs. B keep daily notes on Joseph. A case study will be done on him by the elementary supervisor so that when we meet again she will have had a chance not only to analyze his test scores but also his daily performance in the classroom."

Mrs. S: "Ralph, I must agree with the principal. I believe that he is working to really help Joseph. Let's give Mrs. B a chance."

Mr. S: "I can't agree, and I hope you're not making a big mistake."

This case is unusual as the hostility of both parents is very evident. The directness of Mr. S, "You are forcing me to accept your point of view," speaks of an urgency that requires immediate action on the part of the counselor.

Both parents "came on strong" right from the beginning of the conference. Evidently they had planned beforehand just how they were going to get a teacher change for their child.

If the principal had not taken the time to carefully review the permanent record folder and to make a number of phone calls, he would have been swamped by their presentation.

Unfortunately, distress signals of this type are sometimes ignored by the schools and the situation easily deteriorates. A parent in this state of mind can create further conflicts in his child's mind and he can go to the superintendent of schools for an administrative decision on changing teachers.

The principal could easily have created a confrontational situation, but instead he sought to bring about a tentative solution to the problem with a planned, structured follow-up.

This case pinpoints the need to have teachers and administrators trained to work with distressed and aggressive parents in such a way that a reasonable solution to the problem will result.

The principal was aware that the turning point in the conference occurred when Mrs. S stated to her husband that she agreed with the principal.

The principal sensed from the beginning of the meeting that Mrs. S would be more amenable to keeping the recommended teacher than her husband. Actually, up to that point the principal was not certain how the conference would go.

Later conferences were very difficult. However, the direct hostility of the parents was not evident.

A Parent's Confusion in Role Identification

Case no. 139J (nonconfrontational)

Principal: "Good morning, Mrs. J, you called concerning your boy, Tom."

Parent: "Yes, I have some real concerns about the school. First I want permission to have Tom take his physical education classes with his friend Bill. You must remember how you refused to put my Tom in Bill's class. Well, this has caused Tom to get very upset about school and I don't see why, at least when Bill takes gym, Tom can't be with him."

Principal: "Do you recall when you originally asked that the boys be placed together? I checked with the teachers and they said that Bill and Tom are too dependent on each other and should be separated. Well, I did arrange for both classes to have lunch and playground at the same time, but that is as far as I can go."

Mrs. J: "I don't understand how teachers can be so insensitive to children today. You'd think that I was asking for the moon. Do you know that the teacher on lunchroom duty yesterday punished Tom on the say so of another boy? I am very concerned about this as I happen to know that this boy is a liar. Tom was hit by Michael and when Tom went to Mrs. Y, his teacher, Michael followed and the teacher made Tom stand in the corner as punishment. Tell me, aren't teachers trained to know how and when to punish children?"

Principal: "I spoke to the three boys involved. The boys admitted to me that Steven hit Tom and that when Tom went to Mrs. Y to report this, Michael went along. Tom was not clear on what Mrs. Y said to him, but Michael stated that Mrs. Y told both boys to stop fighting and to sit down. I mention this because Mrs. Y said that this is what happened. She was concerned when I told her that you were coming in because she saw this as a minor incident."

Mrs. J: "My Tom came home so upset that he doesn't want to go to school anymore. Maybe the teacher doesn't think it's important; however, Tom now is emotionally upset. He said to me, 'That teacher is real sick.' "

Principal: "Does Tom talk quite a bit about the things that Michael does in school?"

Mrs. J: "Yes, and Michael lives down the block from us. I try to keep the boys apart."

Principal: "I mention this because I know from Tom's homeroom teacher that the boys don't get along well. I also talked with the safety patrol girl who was on duty at that time and she said that no child was standing against the wall. Mrs. J, is it possible that Tom projected his concerns about Michael to the point where he became unclear about what actually happened?"

Mrs. J: "Yes, now that we are talking about the incident, I would say that Tom probably decided that it would be better if he was not seated near Michael and maybe in his mind he removed himself from the source of trouble. Isn't that a better decision than what the teacher told him to do? I don't see why children can't change their seats in the lunchroom when they want to."

Principal: "We feed one thousand children in four shifts. I can assure you that if we let children select their own places we would have a very difficult situation on our hands. You do raise an interesting point when you wonder if Tom made a better decision than the teacher."

Mrs. J: "I'm really concerned whether teachers are trained to know how and when to punish children. It seems to me that teachers make decisions without taking into consideration what childern are telling them."

Principal: "I know that as a parent you always differentiate the world of Tom from your world. I'm sure that as you look back upon your childhood you remember when you playacted situations which may have become very real to you."

Mrs. J: "Yes, I guess I did."

Principal: "Certainly we all, as children, engage in fantasy. This is part of being a child. However, as adults we separate the two worlds. Also as adults we make decisions based upon our years of experience."

Mrs. J: "This may be so, but when do you take the word of the child against the word of the teacher?"

Principal: "I would see this in a different light. The teacher works with many different children each day and she brings to the teaching situation her experiences, insights and judgments. The student reinterprets the relationship in light of his own experiential background. In most cases, the flow of communications works well. When it doesn't, then a parent conference is in order."

Mrs. J: "Well, I can see that you have many problems with children in this school."

It is obvious that Mrs. J places the word of her son above that of the teacher in this situation.

Parent confusion resulting from an unclear picture of the child's world and frame of reference as compared to the adult's world and that frame of reference is not uncommon today. I interpret this as causing part of the lack of understanding prevalent among many parents concerning the disciplining of their children.

It is also plain that when the principal mentioned that the safety patrol girl saw no child standing by the wall, the parent rationalized her son's statement into a moral decision that she would like to believe he made. This kind of naive thinking is also part of the confusion found among some parents as they view their offspring as little adults rather than children.

The parent's changing the subject in order to talk about teacher training and teacher awareness pinpoints the difficulties that surround a strained parent conference. An anxious parent will jump from one complaint to another in rapid succession in such a way that an untrained teacher-counselor may become rattled.

The counselor in working in such a tense situation does well to realize the many limitations placed upon the conference by the mother's preconceived notions of her son's "rightness" and the teacher's "lack of understanding."

The counselor would be unwise at that point to pursue some of the mother's concerns in depth as the parent is in no psychological state to accept the situation as it now exists. It is more profitable to follow up in the classroom as the teacher works directly with the children.

The conference notes, of course, should be shared with the teacher so that the teacher may have an opportunity to gather information and to develop an approach to meet the parent at a later conference.

An Angry Parent and His Real Concern

Case no. 870C (nonconfrontational)

Principal: "Hello, Mr. C, it's nice to see you again."

Parent: "You won't think it's so nice after I tell you why I'm here. I'm fed up with cut-up calendar this year. It's terrible! Nobody in his right mind would allow for all those days off from school, and now you're permitting half days for conferences. The conference is a waste of time. What do you expect to accomplish in fifteen minutes?"

Principal: "Yes, I agree that the calendar this year has been cut up. The Jewish holidays came so early this year that we have had two and three-day school weeks. However, both of us would agree that it is important to close school on these days. The real problem is that we have had a great deal of student illness and now we are having two half days for parent-teacher conferences."

Parent: "Yes, that's so. Why do we have to have these conferences now? Can't we just give out the report card as we have done in the past?"

Principal: "Actually, the new reporting system is geared to having a parent-teacher conference the first session to explain to the parent on a one-to-one basis the reasons for the marks on the cards. The second report-card marking period is so arranged that the card will be sent home."

Parent: "But that doesn't explain why a fifteen-minute period is set aside rather than thirty or more minutes. It seems to me that this is a waste of time."

Principal: "Studies have shown that a fifteen-minute conference is sufficient for the average session. However, teachers are scheduling the more involved conference either at the end of the conference time or in the evening so that more time is available."

Parent: "This is just another one of the school district's mistakes. I can see the foul-ups with the buses and the inconvenience for the working mother. Actually, with the school tax as it is, both parents have to go to work to support the schools."

Principal: "Schools have always taken into consideration the working mother. One reason why an alternate time is allowed and this time is often in the evening is to accommodate the working mother. I'm sure that you would agree with me that if schools find a one-to-one meeting more satisfying for parents, then we would want to do the same."

Parent: "The Civic Association, of which I am a paid-up member, has been listening to excuses from the school administration now for three years.

"The last blow that the administration dealt was to announce over the Christmas vacation that some of our children had to be placed on double session as of February 1st because of a population buildup. Now come on, do you really mean to sit there and tell me that the board of education didn't know that the schools would be overcrowded?

"The civic association will actively campaign against certain board members and, I can assure you, put pressure on incompetent school administrators."

Principal: "Mr. C, I can assure you that the board of education was very concerned about the population buildup and the school administrators tried to fix up school and class size as quickly and as efficiently as possible. Unfortunately people are moving into our school district from the city at a phenomenal rate.

"The administration hoped to maintain the same school population as last year, but they could not and probably this summer more changes will be called for."

Parent: "Then let the public know early enough so that we can protest! The civic association is planning appropriate pressure if we have another board of education donnybrook."

Principal: "I can assure you, Mr. C, that as we learn about a population buildup everybody will at least be alerted."

Parent: "Well, I'm still dissatisfied; however, I know that you are a little more aware of how we feel about the lack of communication in this school district."

Principal: "I do appreciate your coming and my door is always open to you. Please don't hesitate to drop in or call so that we may keep in touch."

The forcefulness of Mr. C's presentation could easily have brought about a confrontational situation. Fortunately, the principal did not meet the parent head-on. He utilized a dialogue approach so that Mr. C could express his grievances and yet be informed about some of the pressing problems of a growing district.

It is interesting to note that Mr. C readily utilizes his connection with the civic association as a threat to the principal.

The principal, a veteran of suburban pressures, does not respond in anger, but he does inform the parent of the population buildup and the consequent frustrations of this kind of situation.

One of Mr. C's concerns, although not mentioned by him, is that his working wife has difficulty taking care of the children when school schedules accommodate the holidays and provide for conference time during the regular school week.

The principal has learned that an angry parent will present him with a concern that is sometimes a subterfuge for what really is bothering him. He listens more to the feeling tone of the parent's presentation than to the actual meaning of the words spoken.

The principal is very careful all through the dialogue to be informative and matter of fact without antagonizing the parent. In this way further dialogues and understandings will be possible.

CHAPTER FOUR

The Confrontational Approach:

Head-on Conflict

Head-on conflict meetings are the most frustrating and the most exhausting that principals and teachers face. In the following confrontational cases, material is presented which clearly indicates that nobody really wins a school argument when parents leave a conference angry and dissatisfied.

It is important for the reader to analyze these dialogues and to isolate some of the just concerns that the parents have. It is also important for the reader to think through the approaches used by both the principal and the teacher because these cases obviously do not reach working agreements.

School men realize that even if they are fifty percent or even one hundred percent correct, when parents angrily leave a conference, it has been a failure.

In the case of the second conference described, "The Class Changes Teachers," the teacher not only isolated the goodwill of the parents but turned the class against her. I believe in this case the principal should have taken a firmer hand with the teacher so she would have understood from the start that such high-handed methods only end in negative feelings.

Hopefully, these confrontational conferences will help the reader gain further insights into the inherent problems that result from a head-on conflict situation.

A Parent with Deep Negative Feelings

Case no. 770B

The two confrontation conferences that follow indicate the kind of "I win, you lose" type of thinking that is part of many confrontation meetings. Unfortunately the aftereffects of such meetings sour school relationships for years to come.

One baffling and yet fascinating case conference concerned a student whom teachers classified as a restless, anxious and pressured child.

Michael's problem was accentuated by the fact that he had recently transferred from a nearby parochial school. He found that the public schools permitted him to move about and to speak out more. These changes made it difficult for him to settle into a different kind of situation.

An additional concern in this case revolved around the fact that the boy's father was an articulate, professional educator who cast himself in the role of a critic of the local school system.

One of the more difficult situations that the suburban teacher meets is a conference with a parent who is also a teacher. Often the teacher turned parent has difficulty in separating the two roles.

In the case of Mr. B we have a unique situation where the parent not only fails to differentiate his role as father from schoolman but also does not see his son as part of a larger, cooperative school enterprise.

The school principal first met Michael's parents when his first grade teacher spanked him in front of the class for misbehaving. Both parents asked that the boy be immediately transferred to another room and that the teacher be removed from her job. The parents indicated the teacher they wanted for Michael, and they said that if the principal did not have the other teacher removed they would go directly to the board of education.

The principal held several meetings with the parents explaining to them that he was working with the teacher but that their severe demands did not fit the current situation. The parents, although adamant in their demands and uncompromising at first in their approach, eventually did relent. However, they made it clear to the principal that they would insist on "quality education for their child."

Michael's teacher in the next grade attempted to win over the parents by asking them to come in for a conference early in the term. This enabled the parents to express their feelings about school. Unfortunately, the parents listed a set of conditions that had to be met if they were to allow the child to remain in this particular class. The teacher listened and it appeared as though the conference ended on a positive note.

Two days later Mrs. B arrived at school with her husband. Both parents were noticeably disturbed. They demanded to know why they had not been notified by the principal that their son had been punished in school.

The principal explained to them that he did not know what they were referring to, because the principal is not told every time a child is punished in school.

At that point, Mrs. B explained that if Michael had been transferred last year to another room this would not have happened.

A meeting was set up for the following day with the teacher so that the parents could learn more of what had happened.

The next day, Miss C, Michael's teacher, the principal and Mr. and Mrs. B met. Miss C explained that after she had without success repeatedly told Michael to stop chewing gum, she had him place the gum on his nose for the rest of the school day.

The parents became enraged and accused Miss C of inflicting corporal punishment on their child and humiliating him before his classmates.

After a considerable amount of shouting and cross accusations, the principal managed to get the meeting back to order. He told the parents that if Michael was to be helped, everybody would have to stop yelling.

Miss C presented the father with test scores, class papers and anecdotal records that she had accumulated since the beginning of the school year. She mentioned Michael's maturation problem which his earlier teachers had entered in their yearly reports.

Mr. B was skeptical and quite defensive, stating that the school was not acting in good faith, that the teacher was not qualified to teach and that Miss C repeatedly struck his boy in the face. He charged that the teacher was forcing his boy into "an academic straightjacket" and that his son was "pressured by an overzealous teacher." "The oppressive homework and the excessive emphasis in the classroom on reading, writing and arithmetic rather than on finding oneself is abominable," he exclaimed. "More time should be devoted to art and less time to the academic areas of the curriculum," he stated.

At this point Miss C began to cry and said that she never laid a hand on Michael.

The principal interceded, telling Mr. B that he would request that the superintendent work with him to further clarify the whole case.

Mr. B agreed to this arrangement. The next day, the principal received a phone call from Mr. B. He stated that he had changed his mind. He did not want the superintendent to attend any conferences because it would be a black mark on his son's record. He stated that he was aware how schools blacklisted certain students and he did not want this to happen to his son.

The principal took issue with the father, but after some time he stated that the request would be granted.

The principal did have an opportunity to review some of the teacher's comments on Michael's permanent record card. He found that teachers believed Michael had low vitality, sought out his father when the going became difficult and, although very fond of art, rebelled against art lessons when his father arranged for them. Teachers further stated that Michael was in a pressure cooker at home and that his parents should let him develop at his own rate. The conference notes showed that Mr. B wanted his son to become either an artist or an art teacher like himself.

The next conference that the principal had with Mr. and Mrs. B presented an opportunity to tell the parents about the trends indicated in the past parent conferences. The principal suggested that Mr. B talk to Michael about the importance of the academic subjects and assured them that Miss C would be reminded about Michael's keen awareness of art.

At that point Mr. B demanded to have his son's class changed before any further damage was done. Both Mr. and Mrs. B left the conference stating that they expected the principal to notify them of the pending class change.

The next few weeks were difficult ones. The principal did not call the parents. Michael increased in his antagonism toward school.

He began to show less self-control. He constantly rocked in his seat, played with objects in his desk, ran around the room and stuck his tongue out at the teacher. The weekly progress reports that the parents asked for were usually thrown in the basket by Michael while some became paper airplanes.

The teacher and the principal had an emergency meeting to find out what should be done with an already disintegrating situation. It was evident that Michael could not be permitted to continue like this in the classroom and yet it was seen that if the parents were called in they would only become more antagonistic.

It was agreed that Michael had been placed on a high-tension wire and that all parties concerned should disengage and try to let him relax as much as possible.

At about this time, Mrs. B's brother died and the family went to Ohio for the funeral.

Michael was out of school for one week and when he came back he seemed to be calmer. This change in pace helped the teacher gain her composure.

Mr. B called the principal the first day Michael arrived back at school requesting additional homework. The principal told Mr. B that he would gladly send some home. Mr. B then requested that his son have Mrs. L as a teacher for the next school year. The principal told Mr. B that requests for special placement were not accepted because this would result in an avalanche of calls and concerns from many parents. Mr. B became very upset. He stated that the principal was trying to intimidate him. He threatened to go directly to the president of the board of education and have the principal fired.

The next day the principal received a call from the president of the board of education saying that Mr. B had quite a concern and that if a change in class would solve his problem, it would be wise to do so.

The principal asked the superintendent of schools to call a meeting with Mr. and Mrs. B so that the situation could be clarified by somebody higher than the principal.

The superintendent called a meeting the following week. At that meeting, the superintendent quoted from the permanent record folders stressing teacher observations. They stated that Michael leaned on his father during times when pressure built up and that he imagined many concerns. The superintendent spoke about a balanced curriculum and the need for the academic subjects as well as the creative ones.

Mr. B became quite emotional during this meeting. As soon as the superintendent finished talking he blurted out that everybody was ganging up on him. He accused the principal of siding with the teacher against him.

"The trouble with you principals is that you're insensitive to parents. You use your authority to cover up your mistakes.

"You are taking this opportunity to chastise me because I have questioned your authority."

The principal began to realize that he must have struck a very sensitive nerve.

How much frustration, pent up for how long, was released at this point?

What had this teacher suffered at the hands of a principal?

The principal suggested that Mr. B talk with his son and try to get his boy to understand the importance of the academic subjects while at the same time he promised Mr. B that he would work with Miss C so that she could further relate to Michael's interest in art.

Mr. and Mrs. B turned to the superintendent and thanked him for taking the time to talk with them and, without glancing in the principal's direction, stalked out of the office.

The parents completely withdrew after this conference and Michael continued to relate in a negative way both to his teacher and to his studies. He showed an interest only in his art lessons.

It is possible that only a confrontational situation could result from these meetings. A parent with these deep negative feelings toward the public schools and the school authorities would be triggered into striking out at the least provocation.

Mr. B's unrealistic approach in demanding teacher changes, as he stated, "before any further damage be done," and his presenting a set of conditions if he was to allow his child to remain in the class, highlight his confusion.

The accessibility of the president of the board of education to a parent is common. Unfortunately, some board presidents and board members take each complaint that they receive directly to the principal or to the teacher. When this occurs, the board member overrules the professional line and staff organization and he becomes the judge and jury.

The principal later found that the father had received a number of negative evaluations of his own teaching from his school administrator. This information came into the principal's possession after the completion of these conferences. It is doubtful that the principal could have averted the confrontation, but he might have deferred the meetings and asked for a professional team to evaluate the case.

Some school districts do have personnel within their system or from neighboring systems who can be drawn upon to study such a problem.

When such an approach is used, it does place Michael's problem before what the B's might consider a more objective group.

It is well to remember that not all parent-teacher conferences produce positive results. It is unrealistic to think that every parent problem has a solution.

As the students say, "You can't win them all."

The Class Changes Teachers

Case no. 982R (confrontational)

One of the difficulties that besets a class is a teacher change in mid-year. The adjustments that are needed are minimized when there is a similarity between the incoming and the outgoing teacher.

Unfortunately, it is not always possible to match teacher types that well and one of the unusual confrontational situations encountered grew out of such a change.

Mrs. M had an opportunity to work with the outgoing teacher actively in the classroom for one week. During that time she had a chance to observe the outgoing teacher's style, the children's work habits and in general familiarize herself with the school's operation.

Mrs. M commented to the principal that although her style was more direct and vocal than the other teacher's she thought that the children would adjust easily.

Shortly after Mrs. M took charge of the class, parents began to call the principal complaining that the teacher yelled at the children. Some of the children became uneasy about the new teacher and the absence rate in the class began to rise.

The principal observed the teacher and he found that she did speak in a rasping, scratching voice and that when several of the boys were unruly, she would punish the entire class by giving the students a written assignment.

The classroom problem was accentuated by the hostile reaction of Steven to the replacement teacher. This hostility was present with the former teacher but now it emerged in a very defiant way.

Steven reacted to Mrs. M by whistling when the teacher gave a spelling, dictation lesson. When Mrs. M told Steven to stop he retorted, "make me, fatso." The teacher responded by dragging Steven into the hall and calling the principal.

When the principal called the parents in, they stated, with considerable annoyance, that their son was miserable in class because the teacher yelled at the children all day.

"Why, Steven got a 49 on the arithmetic test and he is quite upset," stated Mrs. R.

Mrs. R insisted that Steven be changed to another class.

The principal spoke at length about Steven's restless behavior and his lack of respect for the teacher.

The principal told Mr. and Mrs. R he would observe Steven in the class and arrange a meeting with the teacher in the very near future.

The following week the principal sat with both parents and Mrs. M. The principal stated that during his classroom observations Steven constantly made animal-like noises, jumped out of his seat and ran about the room aimlessly. Furthermore, Steven appeared to be unaware that the principal was in the room.

Mrs. R became noticeably angry and stated that her son was very bright and that he had been incorrectly placed in school. She said that the teacher was not sufficiently challenging him.

The meeting ended with the agreement that the school psychologist work with Steven.

The next day the school psychologist did a series of tests on Steven. That afternoon Mrs. R called the principal and said that the school psychologist was not to touch Steven as she had not given permission for any tests. Mrs. R stated that she would have her private psychologist consult the principal for he had been working with Steven for the past year.

The principal registered surprise because no mention had been made of outside psychological help for Steven.

The private psychologist did send his findings to the school and it gave the principal an opportunity to have the school psychologist meet with Mr. and Mrs. R.

The psychologist's conference with Mr. and Mrs. R left much to be desired. When the school psychologist suggested that the parents were confusing their own problems with Steven's and that their misdirected hostility toward the schools was a factor in their son's adjustment they asked why the school officials were harassing them.

During this meeting Mrs. R admitted that she did give Steven too much latitude as a very young child. She related how she would laugh when at five years old he would take her lit cigarette from the ashtray and parade in front of guests puffing away. She said that Steven would go to any extent to get attention. He was the youngest child and the last they expected to have, so she felt he should be allowed to do many things that her other children were not permitted to do.

The next day, enraged, Mr. and Mrs. R stormed into the principal's office and accused Mrs. M of using corporal punishment on their son and humiliating him before the class. They insisted that if their boy was not changed to another class they would go directly to the board of education.

The teacher was asked to come into the meeting so that the parents' accusations of corporal punishment and humiliation could be clarified.

Mrs. M stated that Steven had answered her back and she had made him stand in the corner with a piece of masking tape over his mouth for the rest of the day. The teacher then accused the parents of not bringing up their child properly and stated that they were responsible for his blatant, defiant behavior.

The parents left quite angry.

Steven did not come to school for the rest of the week. When he did come in, Mrs. R presented the principal with a letter from her son's pediatrician which stated that the boy's mental health was being impaired by an insensitive teacher. A copy of the letter had been sent to the president of the board of education.

Evidently, Mrs. R had spoken to her son as he behaved very well for the next few days.

The principal spent the next week having separate meetings with the parents on the one hand and with Mrs. M on the other. He was not able to get the parents and the teacher to sit down together, but he did get certain agreements worked out at the different meetings.

Mrs. R said that she realized she vacillated between beating Steven to get him to do what she wanted and allowing him to do what he pleased. She agreed that a degree of consistency was needed and that her husband should take a more active part in disciplining their son.

Mrs. M had a chance to talk about her approach with children. She believed that children have too much freedom today and that if the parents don't teach them respect the schools must. The principal talked about child growth and development in a contemporary setting, but Mrs. M maintained her position.

At the end of the school year Steven had settled down due to the intervention of his father, and Mrs. M accepted a teaching position in another school district.

It is evident that Mrs. M precipitated a confrontational situation by reacting forcefully. She further aggravated the situation by accusing the parents of not bringing up their child properly.

Unfortunately, Mrs. M's approach to the class did produce a degree of anxiety that could have been avoided if she had more awareness of the kind of school setting she was working in. This awareness can be cultivated to some extent; however, contemporary attitudes of viewing the student as an active member of the class who will voice opinions and grow in a creative atmosphere must also be understood. This understanding is part of the individual's basic makeup and no amount of sensitivity training can change a teacher's fundamental outlook toward children.

It is interesting to note that once Mr. R took an active role in disciplining his boy, changes occurred. Too often in suburbia the disciplining of the boy is left to the mother. As a result, an already hard-pressed mother is faced with another chore. Now she has to assume the traditional father's role as well as be the family chauffeur, financier and household manager.

In a suburban culture where the adult male is seen mostly by his children on weekends, he would do well to take advantage of his male uniqueness and project a male image, especially to his sons.

The elementary schools can do much for this cultural imbalance by employing more male teachers, especially on the primary level.

CHAPTER FIVE

The Indirect Approach:

The Teacher Listens

as the Problem Is Explored

The two case studies that follow indicate an indirect approach where the teacher permits the parent to talk out her concerns. Both conferences are reenacted many times each day in the nation's schools.

It is important for the reader to understand the approach the teacher uses, because this indirect approach is more and more needed today in a society where people have a need simply to talk out their concerns. The school is in a unique position, being available as a sounding-out post. It is the skillful teacher who permits the parent to talk and then asks the really important questions. In both these case studies, the teacher encouraged the mother to develop her own sound conclusions. In one case, the mother decided to go to the principal while in the other case the parent was guided to see the school psychologist.

The value of studying these conferences is in noting a method where the teacher assumes the role of counselor—one who knows not only when to speak but what to say.

At a time when face-to-face meetings are becoming more frequent both in sensitivity training groups and in parent-teachers' association discussion groups, techniques that enable the parent to talk out her concerns are becoming more valuable in bringing about worthwhile understandings.

Will Mother Accept Bill's Potential?

Case no. 908M

Parent: "I'm Bill's mother. I'm just sick over my son. After I read his report card I just had to talk to you. I know that he is slow, but I'm sure that he can be helped. My husband and I both did well in school. John, Bill's older brother, is on the honor roll in high school. Maybe a tutor will help."

Teacher: "Bill is working at his own rate."

Parent: "The teacher last year said that Bill may have to repeat a grade. This is just what I don't want. Can you help him now?"

Teacher: "Bill grasps things but it takes him a little while. He is coming along."

Parent: "I can't understand why he doesn't do better. I have helped him with his homework. His father has given him extra arithmetic examples to do. It's not that our home isn't stimulating. Why, the house is full of books and interesting things. Maybe I should go to the principal and have some tests given to him. He should do much better."

Teacher: "Bill needs a lot of patience. He does respond to praise. He is a very sweet boy and I enjoy working with him."

Parent: "Bill's situation is tragic. I don't know how to cope with him. We have given him everything possible and he still takes so long to do things."

Teacher: "There are many things that Bill does well. Yesterday he fixed the window shade. Nobody in the room could figure out what was wrong with it.

Parent: "I expect Bill to learn how to read and to write well. When I hear that he is two years below grade level, I become desperate. At this rate he will never be able to get into college. I begin to blame myself. Where have I gone wrong? What have I not given him?"

Teacher: "Did Bill bring home the mother's day present that he made for you?"

Parent: "Yes, but I would have been prouder if he brought me a good arithmetic paper. His brother works with him after school but it doesn't help.

"Maybe if I go to the principal he will help me see what is wrong with Bill."

Teacher: "I'll arrange for a meeting with the principal."

The conference with Bill's mother was one where the teacher gave Mrs. M an opportunity to express her concerns. It is evident that the mother has a much higher expectation level for Bill than is realistic. In a society where academic achievement is a mark of success, it is difficult to accept intellectually limited children on their own ability level. The emphasis on getting into college and the professions tends to belittle the other areas of performance where some children excel.

It is possible that Bill may have mechanical skills that would enable him to do well in some of the trades. It may be quite difficult, however, if this be the case, for Bill's mother to accept her son in a nonprofessional job.

Unfortunately, many children are pushed into college, only to drop out, who should have been encouraged to attend a trade school where they would be able to learn a much-needed skill and be better able to adjust to life.

Later meetings with the teacher and the principal were so structured that Mrs. M had a chance to realize that Bill was developing at his own rate even if it was slower than his older brother.

Mrs. M never did accept that Bill, although developing at his own rate, may not enter college or go into the professions.

Hopefully, this understanding, so desperately needed, may come later in high school when the guidance counselor will be working with Bill. His mother then may be more aware of her son's potential.

The Overactive Child

Case no. 201S (indirect)

Teacher: "Good morning, Mrs. S. I'm glad to see you; however, I did not expect you to drop in to see me today."

Parent: "I just had to see you as soon as possible. I hope you don't mind but I have so many concerns about Paula."

Teacher: "That's quite alright, I'm always glad to see you."

Parent: "Paula has been coming home with a great deal of homework. When I questioned her she revealed that most of it was work that she failed to complete in class. I go along with you on having her do this work at home, but I am concerned about why she does not complete more in school. Am I correct in assuming it is because she is very easily distracted?"

Teacher: "Well, Paula is rather alert."

Parent: "Every teacher has noted that Paula is bright, but she has difficulty sitting still and minding her own business. I fear that if we cannot help her overcome this soon it will be too late. I recognize this problem can be answered only in a special class."

Teacher: "Paula has many interests."

Parent: "Yes, maybe this is part of her problem. Would it be possible for you to isolate her? Maybe if you placed her desk by yours she would not be so easily distracted by her friends. I don't mean this to be a punishment but as a way of helping her be less distracted. At home I insist that she do her homework in her room without any interruptions at all."

Teacher: "I have found Paula to be very creative and I do carefully plan her time."

Parent: "If this is not her problem maybe we should look deeper. For instance, she constantly moves about. Her papers are so sloppy that I wonder . . ."

Teacher: "Possibly the school psychologist could help. He would be glad to talk to you."

Parent: "That's a good idea. I wonder if Paula's problem is not emotional. I have been planning to take her to a good pediatrician. Maybe he will find some kind of imbalance somewhere."

Teacher: "How does Paula react at home?"

Parent: "Paula can never sit still. She flits from one thing to the next. She begins a job and then she tires of it. Why, she has so many projects that our house is just full of all kinds of unfinished things. She doesn't seem to be able to hold on to friends either.

"I don't know where I have failed. I have tried hard to be a real friend to her and not have her see me as her mother. I don't know, maybe it would be well if the school psychologist works with her."

Teacher: "I'm sure that this can be arranged. In the meantime feel free to come in to see me anytime."

Parent: "Thank you, I certainly will. And I do appreciate the fact that you don't mind when I call you up at night and talk to you about Paula."

The teacher, having created an accepting conference situation, has permitted Mrs. S to talk out her concerns. While the parent talks about careless school work and her child's being restless, the teacher encourages the parent to think about the services of the school psychologist.

Many parents need someone to talk to. Sometimes a parent will talk out a school situation to a neighbor. The parent may come away feeling better or she may be triggered off by the neighbor's concerns to form a committee, start a petition or be at the next board of education meeting.

This kind of over-the-backyard-fence discussion many times has repercussions which are felt at the next P.T.A. meeting where a group of parents ask to form a study group to find out what is going on in a curriculum area or to better study the buses as they pick up children in the morning.

The value of the parent's presenting her concerns to the teacher is that the parent is placing the problem where it belongs, in the school. The teacher in this real-life situation now may take action on the concern rather than have a clothes-line interpretation of the problem intermixed with many other neighbors' concerns.

The skilled teacher realizes that the time taken to help resolve a pressing parent problem saves administrators and the child's future teachers many hours of conference time.

CHAPTER SIX

The Direct Approach:

Transmitting Information

to the Parents

The case conferences that follow present the direct approach where the educator "tells" the parent. In both conferences the educators tend to "talk down" to the parent, an approach which unfortunately is all too common in educational circles.

It is important for the reader to ask himself why both the principal and the teacher take this approach. Is it because the educators are concerned about facing the real problems presented by the parents? Are the educators so insensitive to the concerns of the parent that they are unable to discuss the real issues? Whatever the conclusions of the reader, it is well to analyze this approach used by many educators which "turns off" parents.

It is also interesting to compare the direct approach used by the schoolman with the direct approaches used by parents in chapter three. In all cases the approach leaves very little to be negotiated by the other party.

The practical value of studying such an approach is to realize that in any productive discussion there must be room for accommodation, that is, there must be some give and take on the part of all concerned.

The aware educator knows that the parent must leave the conference feeling a degree of satisfaction. If the parent is "put down," the result of the meeting will be one of resentment and hostility.

In these two cases the educator is the "expert" who imparts knowledge and information to the parent. The educator could just as easily have sent a report home, since in both cases he is conducting a virtual monolgue.

The Principal Has an Answer for Everything

Case no. 103G

Principal: "Good morning, Mrs. G. I haven't seen you since you went back to teaching. How do you like high school?"

Mrs. G: "Oh, I love it, but I'm concerned about the school lunches for my daughter, Alice."

Principal: "I imagine that you are as impressed as I am that we now feed one thousand children. Can you visualize all those students going through four lunch shifts in a two-hour period? The schools are certainly offering an unusual service for the public."

Mrs. G: "I suppose so; Alice has complained that the lunch portions are too small."

Principal: "The head cook is very cognizant of the fact that fifth and sixth grade students are physically bigger, and she does see that they get more food on their tray. I am sure that you can appreciate the problem though of adjusting tray sizes as children pour through the lunch line. Do you realize that one student goes through the lunch line every ten seconds? Why, the split timing is so precise in the lunchroom that if a class is just two minutes late a whole lunch shift is thrown off schedule."

Mrs. G: "Well, I guess so. . . . I did want to mention too that Alice has been complaining about getting too much homework."

Principal: "Homework is worked out by each teacher keeping in mind school-district policy. As you know, a fifth grade student should receive forty minutes of homework per night. However, we both are aware that this is an average figure and it does not take into account individual cases. Alice may take sixty minutes for the same assignment that somebody else in the class would take thirty minutes to do. I do believe that the teacher tries to take all these factors into consideration when she gives a homework assignment."

Mrs. G: "But Alice has been taking about two-and-a-half hours per night for homework."

Principal: "I would suggest that you check her work habits first. Some children sit down in front of the TV set with a bowl of popcorn or fruit. Some will hurry the assignment during the commercial. Other students take breaks and talk on the phone. Yes, I would suggest that you look into Alice's work-study habits. Do you have a place for Alice to work where she has plenty of light and where it is quiet?"

Mrs. G: "Oh yes, Alice has her own room."

Principal: "That's fine! The first requisite for good homework is a room of one's own. Then I would suggest good lighting, proper heating and no distractions."

Mrs. G: "I did want to mention that Mr. G and I have a concern about how Mr. X teaches his class."

Principal: "I do know that Alice has taken advantage of the afterschool math club that Mr. X teaches. I think this is a good idea. We both know how important it is for Alice to get a firm background in math today."

Mrs. G: "I wasn't really concerned about the math club. I was more concerned about how Mr. X teaches reading."

Principal: "I'm glad you mentioned that. I worked with Mr. X just the other day on his attempts to perfect his individualized reading program. He has been using the school district's reading levels to perfect his individualized reading approach with children. Mrs. G, I tell you that individualization is the final development in education. Imagine how you and I taught all children the same way. Isn't that a far cry from the small group and individualized instruction that we have today? Yes, Mrs. G, I'm glad that you brought your concern to me for I can assure you that with the new reading program and the instructional team that works with Mr. X, he does solve these instructional problems."

Mrs. G: "Well, thank you for your time."

Principal: "Thank you, Mrs. G, and please don't hesitate to come in to see me anytime that you have a problem. Our school prides itself on the fact that parents are kept informed on all school activities."

The approach that the principal used with Mrs. G could be considered humorous if it wasn't so widespread in educational circles.

The principal probably was as far removed from the concerns the mother presented as could be. He had an answer for everything and the parent hardly had a chance to express her real concerns about the school's functioning and the classroom teacher.

Mrs. G in jumping from one concern to another was not only attempting to get a word in edgewise but was also trying to tell the principal her many worries about the school.

A more understanding principal would have permitted her to voice her concerns and would have given her facts pertinent to her questions.

A follow-up meeting with the teacher would have given the principal a better understanding of the student's homework assignment and the reading program in Mr. X's room.

The principal would have done well to ask Mrs. G if she had spoken to the teacher first about some of her classroom concerns.

A proper procedure would be for the principal to help the parent with her concerns about the lunchroom but to remind the parent that the teacher should be called on to answer instructional questions.

Too often suburban parents go directly to the principal on matters that should be handled on the teacher level.

Some parents reason that if they go "to the top" they will get faster action. They also reason that in so far as the principal is the teacher's supervisor they are placing the teacher in a postion where he may have to modify his approach to the child even if he desires not to.

There is a great need in many suburban communities to spell out the role of the parent so that he better understands the procedures that should be followed for a more effective and efficient school organization. Here is an example of a teacher using the direct approach:

The Teacher as Pedagogue

Case no. 219H (direct)

Teacher: "Mrs. H, I have asked you to come in today because I am very aware that John is not working anywhere near his potential. Actually, he does very little in school except to cause a disturbance in the room."

Parent: "My husband and I have talked about John's school work. John is not being challenged under this new reporting system. He is bored with the new marks. Imagine bringing home an S rather than an 85. Why all incentive is crushed for the child!"

Teacher: "We teachers realize that children grow, learn and mature at different rates. John's evaluation should reflect an understanding of his intellectual, physical, social and emotional growth. The parent conferences will point out to you what your child's potential is in a meaningful way. I will work with John so that he will challenge himself."

Parent: "But, I don't really see . . ."

Teacher: "Mrs. H, I can assure you that John will soon be working at his expected level. This is where he should be functioning. He has the ability, and after he has completed the battery of standardized achievement tests that I have given him we will know more about his placement."

Parent: "You talk about placement, I have a concern about this new program."

Teacher: "The new marking system works hand in glove with the new program. John will be placed on his reading level after the standardized test results are in and we will see that he advances as his ability and his motivation allow him to rather than to lock him into a grade with an 85 that he can easily achieve anyhow. Now, Mrs. H if we can just work together to help John settle down in school a little more."

Parent: "I will deprive him of the cub scouts until he behaves better."

Teacher: "I must take issue with you, Mrs. H. John needs all the social experiences that we can give him. I would encourage his going to the cub scouts just as often as possible. Actually, John's limited social contacts make him a target for the other boys. He doesn't relate well to other children at all. At school we are very concerned about the well-rounded individual and we try to develop experiences for him so that he will become a better citizen."

Parent: "Well, both my husband and I have really been more interested in John's work habits than in his behavior toward other children."

Teacher: "Work habits are important; however, without the ability to get along with other people, John will be most unhappy.

"Just the other day John took a chair and paraded up and down the room with it on his head. Most of the children just ignored him. A few laughed and he continued until I told him to sit down. I would suggest the school psychologist work with him."

Parent: "My husband would never agree."

Teacher: "That's unfortunate; the psychologist is a skilled professional who is able to work with children who have problems. I have had a number of students the psychologist has helped. Sometimes it's just a little insight into their behavior that is necessary. Why don't you speak to your hsuband and see if he will not reconsider?"

Parent: "Well, I'll see; thank you for taking the time to talk with me."

Teacher: "Thank you for coming, Mrs. H. Actually, the parent and teacher conference is most important, and with the new reporting system, teachers have a wonderful opportunity to explain to parents how the new marking system works and parents have an opportunity to ask questions."

The teacher presented her concerns about John to his mother in a forthright way. She tended to be pedantic and although her suggestions were good, the parent was placed on the defensive.

It is obvious that the mother does not agree with the way the teacher is handling John. She further is placing her emphasis on academic achievement while the express purpose of the meeting as called by the teacher is to discuss the emotional and social growth of the student.

The teacher also had the last word and she managed to further instruct the parent as the conference ended.

The teacher would do well to have both the mother and the father in at a meeting where they could discuss John's social problems in the room. In this way there would be no question of one parent communicating the teacher's behavior report to the other parent in a distorted way. This meeting would also give the H's an opportunity to talk out their concerns about the new marking system and possibly to explore John's social behavior.

The immediate reaction on the part of the teacher when mother stated, "I will deprive him of the cub scouts until he behaves better," indicates the level of concern that the teacher has. She is seeking ways to work with the parents to allow John to have wholesome social contacts.

Unfortunately, the very contacts that he needs are being stifled as the mother tries to force better behavior upon her son.

Mr. and Mrs. H need a teacher who can open up a number of areas relating to child growth and development where relationships between academic work and social, emotional growth may be seen in their proper perspective.

CHAPTER SEVEN

The Transplant Problem

The problems presented in this chapter are so common that it is important for both parent and teacher to realize that when a parent moves from a city environment to the suburbs, many adjustments must be made.

Some schools have an orientation program for new parents which includes a home visit by a P.T.A. member, an afternoon meeting with the nurse and the principal at the school, and informational brochures which are sent home. New parent coffee klatches are arranged where parents may ask questions and receive an orientation to the school and to the community. Generally these coffee klatches are held in an established neighbor's home and they are especially effective when a new section of a housing development opens.

In the case of Mrs. J, the school principal and the supervisor have given her an opportunity to ask many questions and to air her concerns. Unfortunately, time does not always permit this kind of dialogue. As a result many hidden resentments smolder and find a way back into the school in a more aggravated form.

A Well-Informed Parent

Case no. 628J

Principal: "Good morning, Mrs. J. I would like to introduce Miss R, our elementary supervisor. I understand that you have some concerns about your daughter, Susan."

Mrs. J: "Yes, I have many things on my mind. We recently

moved here from Queens and, for one, I'm confused about how children are grouped in this school."

Principal: "We have organized our classes so that the range of abilities in each room is narrowed. Some classes have a top cluster where children may progress at a faster rate while some classes have a low cluster to permit for more remedial work. All classes have a range of abilities. In this way no class is typed as the slow class or the fast class."

Mrs. J: "This gives the teacher enough time perhaps to work with what is almost an individual problem. Where most of the children fit into one category, can the teacher work with an individual problem? Will she have time?"

Miss R: "Hopefully, all our teachers individualize instruction to meet the needs of each child, regardless of which group the teacher has. What we hope to accomplish with this particular type of grouping is to narrow the range so that there won't be as many differences in a room."

Mrs. J: "I have a problem about the report card. Is this the reporting method that you are using?"

Miss R: "Yes, the first and third marking periods are parent-teacher conference times. The second and fourth marking periods utilize a satisfactory, unsatisfactory and needs improvement designation."

Mrs. J: "I see; in other words you have no intention in the future of using marks as we know them, A, B, C and D or 65, 75, 85 or anything like that."

Miss R: "Yes."

Mrs. J: "I see. I always had an objection to what we might call the minor subjects as opposed to the regular scholastic subjects— art, music, physical education. My objection has been in the marking system. It seems unfair to have a child who doesn't draw well marked on the basis of his ability to draw. Not everyone sews well or does physical education well. Would your system eliminate this sort of thing?"

Miss R: "The thinking behind our report card is exactly what you are saying. The child now has a chance because of attitude and participation."

Mrs. J: "I have always felt very strongly about this. Everyone does not perform with the same ability and it just doesn't seem fair that a child receive only a fair mark because he doesn't draw well, sing well or . . ."

Miss R: "But I think in this case we have given him an opportunity to get an outstanding mark; for example, he can be given credit for being creative, for having a good attitude or for trying harder."

Mrs. J: "Well, I think this would be a good thing to explain to the children before they get this report card. It may be an involved thing, but I think it would make everyone happier and avoid unnecessary concerns. There seem to be many concerns here. It would be better if this was explained to the children as well as to the parents."

Miss R: "That's a very good idea."

Mrs. J: "I had another question. I think that penmanship has a lot to do with one's coordination—perhaps particularly a younger child. As people get older their coordination and their handwriting get better. Is it absolutely necessary to mark on penmanship?"

Mrs. R: "Only in that perhaps it would point up to a child that there is need for improvement if that be the case or give the child credit who is trying very hard and doing a fine job. Again, I think the matter of muscular coordination and the matter of maturity are taken into consideration by the teacher."

Principal: "I know that Susan has only been with us for three weeks, but how does she feel about school?"

Mrs. J: "I think she feels a little bit behind. As a matter of fact, there seems to be a large gap between the curriculum here and the curriculum she had in the city—particularly in math. I am not talking about the new math as opposed to the old math, but rather I think she was expected to know at the beginning of this term certain things which she did not know. For instance, as far as I recall she only had to know the multiplication table to five, but in September her new teacher did not take into consideration that she did not know to the nine table. She seemed to think everyone in her class should know it. When I discussed it with her teacher she said, 'Well, I can work with the level of the children who have been here and the fastest children. The others will have to catch up.' This doesn't seem fair to me because even though this community is also in New York state, every area has unfortunately a different curriculum.

I was wondering what was being done for the child who was behind."

Miss R: "Well, I would certainly say that the fourth grade curriculum throughout the year will be working with multiplication and division facts. Susan will constantly be working with these things. I am glad the teacher is aware of the fact that the child didn't have it before. Perhaps you at home could help her a little so that she would feel more comfortable. We certainly will make every effort to let the teacher know and she will give additional help to Susan. The entire year's math curriculum is based on multiplication and division, and the class will be using it constantly."

Mrs. J: "It is very upsetting for a parent, of course talking from my own point of view, to come here from another area and not even know until the school is in session for awhile that my child is so far behind. I think that if there was something, some way . . . perhaps a booklet could be made to inform the parents what the child may be up against when he comes here.

"Of course it would be impossible for this school district to know what is going on in every other school district, and to say that we are doing this, and this is all your child learned and this is what he will have to know.

"I also discovered something else as far as math is concerned. I believe in the second grade this district is doing quarts and pint measurements. My child never had this, not even in third grade and again she found this a burden because she was expected to know it. Would the teacher also be expected to help her in this area?"

Miss R: "Well, measurement again is a topic that repeats itself in every grade. I believe it starts in first grade if not in kindergarten and repeats itself so that students will repeat this unit in the fourth grade, and hopefully at that time Susan will catch up and get the basic facts."

Principal: "Do you have another problem?"

Mrs. J: "Yes, my daughter in the past has fortunately had teachers all of whom have had a great deal of experience either with their own children or as teachers. I would say not one of them has had less than ten years of experience. Now my daughter has a brand-new teacher just out of college. I know that they have to start somewhere. However, it seems to me that a fourth grade student in many cases is already what we call preadolescent and has special problems. I am really doubtful that a twenty-one-year-old girl knows how to handle a person who has special problems. Again, I don't like to criticize anyone who is so young, but I think that she just doesn't have the proper amount of patience for a child this age."

Principal: "This is a good point. In our school district we have a broad range of teaching experience on each staff. We have teachers on our staff who are just out of college, and we have some teachers near retirement. We have men and women teachers on the staff. We try to get teachers from many different parts of the country, so that children are exposed to teachers from various backgrounds. Actually, in a rapid-growth district there will be a certain number of beginning teachers. We have an in-service program for new teachers and Miss R, our elementary supervisor, works with teachers on specific problems.

"Very often a teacher right out of college has a great deal of enthusiasm. She brings with her many creative ideas which are an asset to the staff.

"All teachers, of course, are certified by the state of New York and they come equipped as far as their training goes.

"Did you want to add anything to that Miss R?"

Miss R: "Well, only to say that each teacher has had courses in child psychology and a student-teaching experience which in many cases is on the same grade level in which he is teaching. They do have some idea of what the children are like at this age and what to expect of them.

"I would also like to think that they bring a certain something, a certain freshness and newness that we don't always find in veteran teachers.

"Is Susan your first child?"

Mrs. J: "Yes."

Miss R: "Do you have other children?"

Mrs. J: "No, I don't."

Miss R: "Well, I would like to think as a mother I didn't go wrong with my first child. I think that there is something about that first child that is exciting, fresh and different."

Mrs. J: "There is something else from my own point of view to remember. I think that in everyone there is certainly an awful lot of good and I think that when these conferences are held, it's very necessary to go to the parent with something very positive and nice about the child. It's a little disheartening to be told right away that your child is not as bright as you think she is, although you have been told the last four years that your child is very bright and would even have the opportunity to skip if we stayed in the city. It is very disconcerting to be met immediately with, I don't think your child is so bright. Especially when this is said by a very inexperienced person. The fact that she has been student teaching for a few weeks or a few months is another matter. I think that it is a little difficult to accept the teacher who has not had a great deal of experience. Why is she in a position to say, 'Oh, your child is not as bright as you think she is'? I think it is important to delve a little more deeply into the case of a child who is not performing, if the parent is of the impression . . . of course, I don't know if the teacher has seen the records from the previous school.

"I think it is very wrong particularly for an inexperienced teacher to take this attitude with the parent.

"I suppose we all think our children are bright, but again, you have to be careful with a parent about her child. A teacher must have a more positive attitude when she speaks to the parent because naturally we all think our children are great. This is a very important thing for a teacher to learn. I don't know if this can be called public relations or whether this should be included in a teacher's college work."

Miss R: "It might be a good point for us to include this in our orientation program for new teachers."

Mrs. J: "It's very hard just to speak up . . . all the time that your child is not doing well and should be doing better and could be if a teacher tried. I think there is a basic reason for the child's not performing and I believe you are better off trying to find out what this is."

Principal: "Miss R will meet with Susan's teacher so that we can get a complete picture of her progress. Susan has only been with us for three weeks, and through the reading tests and classroom observations we will get a more complete picture of Susan's work.

"I suggest that you come back in several weeks and talk with

us. Miss R will have additional information and we will be very
pleased to meet with you."

Mrs. J: "Yes, that will be fine."

Principal: "All right. Thank you for coming and we will see you
in a few weeks."

CHAPTER EIGHT

The Follow-up Conference

The follow-up conference is an approach used by the principal who is aware that not only does the parent have many unanswered questions, but that a time lapse of several weeks helps in allowing the parent to think through her position.

Sometimes the follow-up conference permits the principal much needed time to gather data through observations, phone calls, tests, and the like, which will give him a clearer picture of the situation.

The parent, in turn, feels that her concern is being given the needed attention it requires rather than being shelved for an indefinite period.

All too often, principals have dismissed concerns of parents as unnecessary and then have assumed that they will just disappear. However, in a time when communication is so important, a follow-up that is carefully planned is of the utmost importance.

Needless to say, the principal has to be alert not to develop the kind of a relationship where the parent keeps coming back just to have someone with whom to talk. This delicate balance between presenting a clear, objective understanding of a child's problem and creating a clinging-vine dependent parent is a fine line and one that most principals walk each day of the school year.

In this follow-up conference, the principal and the elementary supervisor attempt to be informative without placing the parent in the clinging-vine category.

A Well-Informed Parent

Case no. 628J (nonconfrontational) (continued)

When Mrs. J returned for a follow-up conference several weeks later, she had many of the same unanswered problems presented in Chapter Seven. The supervisor and the principal answered some of her questions; however, there was no indication that the teacher had attempted to contact Mrs. J. It is unfortunate that the teacher did not ask Mrs. J in for a get-together meeting shortly after Susan arrived in her class.

Principal: "Good morning, Mrs. J. How are you?"

Mrs. J: "I'm fine. How are you, Miss R?"

Miss R: "Fine, thank you, and yourself?"

Mrs. J: "My daughter tells me that she's had some kind of test; I believe she called it an achievement test. I also understand that there is another test called an ability test. Could you please explain the difference to me?"

Miss R: "The ability test is called a test of mental maturity and it's an intelligence test. The achievement test is a test that indicates performance in certain subject areas. There isn't too much I can tell you about the achievement test yet because the results have not come back from the test scoring service."

Mrs. J: "I see."

Miss R: "Once the results are back I am sure your daughter's teacher will meet with you and perhaps, if you would like me to be there, we can go over the results and explain them to you."

Principal: "That would be a good idea. The achievement test gives us a rather good indication on this grade level of how well the child is doing with academic skills.

"The mental maturity test doesn't point up achievement but it does point up ability.

"When we compare the ability with the achievement test we have an idea of the child's ability in terms of her achievement."

Mrs. J: "Is it realistic to assume that a child who does well on the ability test will do well on the achievement test?"

Principal: "If we find a very fine ability score, we should find similar results on the achievement test.

"We find consistently that as people come in from the city there is an adjustment period.

"We are talking about our P.T.A. next year working with us on an orientation program for new parents. In this way we hope to allay some of the concerns that parents have in adjusting to a new community.

"It isn't only the adjustment in working out problems within your own neighborhood such as getting to know your neighbors and finding a plumber if your faucet leaks, but also in adjusting your child to school.

"What I am trying to say is that although a child may do very well on the ability tests, the achievement and the classroom tests may not show up as well as we would expect.

"If it is a child that just came in from the city, we would say there is an adjustment period that is taking place.

"There may be many other factors. Very often, we find that work-study skills are not as clearly understood as they should be or occasionally we find a child who has a number of what we commonly call mental blocks."

Mrs. J: "Well, with your past experience with children coming from the city, does this happen often? Do you find a gap in the child's achievement as opposed to her mental maturity? If so, is this because of the difference in the curriculum?"

Miss R: "The achievement tests are nationwide. However, there are certain areas that might be stressed in one school district as opposed to another and these would come about from the diagnosis of the evaluations of the tests."

Mrs. J: "I realize these tests are made by a group of people somewhere in the country. How can they arrive at a test when the curriculum is so different just in New York state alone?"

Miss R: "Through sampling, testing and experimentation they have discovered certain basic concepts and achievements that all children at a certain grade level should have attained. It does not necessarily have to be something that they have specifically been taught. Certain concepts will carry over to another skill."

Mrs. J: "I see."

Miss R: "This gives an overall picture. The test is broad enough to cover the kinds of things that are taught to children in the elementary schools."

Mrs. J: "Is this mark arrived at by taking each category, adding it up and dividing it and getting an average, or is there some other way of marking?"

Miss R: "It is the number of items correct and it's scaled to a percentile. This is done with large samplings nationwide of children who take the test. The number of items correct is scaled according to the child's grade placement so that a fourth grader would be expected to get a certain number right in order to achieve a 50th percentile which is the average for his grade. The fifth grade student would be expected to get more items correct to receive a certain score."

Mrs. J: "Actually a mark may be interpreted differently in different parts of the country."

Miss R: "Right. We find in our school district the average score is a year above the national average."

Mrs. J: "And would an 85 mean that a child is eight-years-old in what he knows?"

Miss R: "An 85 percentile score on the test means that of all the children on that grade level who took that test, 85 percent of the children scored lower than this child scored and 15 percent scored higher."

Mrs. J: "I see. To get back to the bright child, I guess I don't know what is considered a high I.Q., but I have been led to believe that my daughter's is rather high. Now suppose if when she goes on into the next class she takes an achievement test and she still doesn't get what is considered a good score as compared to her intellectual mental maturity. What would this be a reflection of? Would this be a lack of motivation on the child's part? Is she not being stimulated properly?"

Miss R: "This could be. There is always the factor of testing. Children react differently to a test. Some children test well. Some children don't. Some children have learned to pace themselves on a test. When you consider that the test was based on the number of items correct, a child who might work more slowly and more carefully could possibly get a lower score than a child who races through a test almost guessing or taking a chance on an answer. The teacher in diagnosing the test results also has to bear in mind the child and be able to evaluate the results with the child's personality and the child's work habits in mind as well. There can be so many factors that it is difficult to take scores cut and dry and assume that they mean only one thing."

Mrs. J: "We were discussing the grouping procedure at our last conference. How much are these test marks used as a basis for grouping? If a child has a high I.Q. but doesn't perform quite that well in class and he is placed in a low cluster is this not bad for him?

"Perhaps a bright child isn't being stimulated at all. Perhaps he is not being challenged. He may work harder and this may cause him to fall further behind rather than spurring him on."

Miss R: "I would hesitate to make a flat statement. Each teacher teaches at a different rate because of the cluster in her room. Even with the cluster grouping, each class has a wide range of ability. As we said, the teachers are trying to individualize their teaching so that they aren't teaching to the whole class at any particular rate.

"As we arrive at cluster grouping, the test scores are one means of deciding class structure. However, they are only a basis perhaps for the original placement. Teacher judgment is the most important factor in placing children.

"Personality factors are very important. Some children just cannot work together and must be separated."

Mrs. J: "Getting back to my own experience last year and three years before we came here, there were seven third grades averaging almost forty children in a class in that city school. They truly had grouped the children by their own particular ability. There was a slower and a faster class and in a way this makes sense because putting a slower child with a faster child is frustrating for the slower child. He may say to himself, 'I could never keep up with this kid because I know he is smart. There is no point in my trying.'

"This is the way it was when we went to school. There were at least four classes in each grade and each one had a definite group. Of course, I don't say that there weren't smarter children in the fast class. There may also have been some other slower children but it seems to me that this might be a good way of doing it because perhaps you are stimulating each group of children at their own ability rather than trying to have children of several abilities in one class. It seems to have worked well and so I'm partial to it."

Miss R: "Extensive research has been carried on in grouping and probably as much research in the particular area of what we call homogeneous or like grouping as in heterogeneous grouping. Research has not proven one better than the other."

Mrs. J: "I see."

Miss R: "As many favorable reports as you read, you will find as many opposing views and you can find arguments just as good for one as you can for the other."

Mrs. J: "I see."

Principal: "I think another concern with the homogeneous group situation is that very often it becomes a status situation for the children and for the parents. All of us here are parents and we know that the child is a projection of ourselves. If the child is in a top group, then undue pressure can be placed upon the child and a lot of negative learning experiences can develop."

Mrs. J: "Well, what about the child with the high I.Q. who should be achieving? I guess you call this an underachiever. Suppose he is put in the not-so-top group and his teacher is aware of this high I.Q. Don't you think that she would put pressure on that child anyway to achieve more than he is achieving? I guess it's a little difficult for a teacher to see anyone with a so-called good mind who is not using it completely, and it is hard for her not to use pressure. Sometimes you are not accomplishing anything.

"I think that you have to feel out your child and after you have put pressure on him awhile and you haven't accomplished anything, then perhaps you have to try another tack and find something good he is doing to make a fuss over. If you are accomplishing nothing with one method, then it's time to switch to something else. Obviously, constant pressure doesn't work on everyone. Some people do better work under pressure than other people. At the same time you are putting pressure on the parents, and the parents are going home and putting further pressure on the child.

"It is very difficult to be told, 'your child should be doing better and why isn't she?'; when the teacher obviously isn't able to put her finger on the problem, I don't know how the parent can either."

Principal: "Yes, what you are saying is very true. The more instruction is individualized, the better we will be able to identify problems. I think here the teacher attempts to know the child as soon as possible.

"Miss R, I understand you had a chance to observe Susan in the classroom."

Miss R: "Susan is adjusting quite well in the class. She seems to have made friends and is rather happy. I reviewed her reading test. She did well in her comprehension and word-attack work. Perhaps some of those skills that she should have had in her background are a little weak. Perhaps she hasn't done as much with syllabication and some of the other skills that we are working with here."

Mrs. J: "Reading tests were used extensively last year in Susan's school. I don't know if all children brought the tests home, but my daughter was permitted to do so. She came out at eighth and ninth grade level. However, I got the impression from the little I've seen of her teacher this term that Susan is not reading anywhere near this. I am curious to know what could have happened in these few months since school ended in June in the city and school has started here."

Miss R: "Well, none of these reading tests are necessarily coordinated with each other in their rating. These tests are all rated in a different way, so you have to use each one as a frame of reference."

Mrs. J: "I see. We, of course, were informed last June that Susan would go into a rapid class in the city. Children had to be at least two grades in reading level above their grade and had to have at least a 129 I.Q. So, of course, having been told my daughter was eligible for this class and then finding that she's not too much above her grade level here is hard for me to comprehend. How could there be such a vast difference in her ability in one school as opposed to another?"

Miss R: "Well, there is a difference. The sampling here is different from some other places. Our children come to us very highly motivated for learning. Our teachers are always amazed with the readiness with which our children learn things. As a result the curriculum moves along at a very fast pace."

Mrs. J: "Is it safe to assume perhaps in the future when the adjustments have passed, a child with a high I.Q. will do better? In other words, after being in this school district a certain amount of years or months, is it safe to assume she will do better?"

Principal: "Well, this is a very good point. I think it's safe to say that one factor will be taken care of and it's a very big factor. After the child has adjusted to a new school and a somewhat different curriculum and there are still problems in work habits, then we would look into other areas, but as we said before, the whole problem of adjustment is most important. I would suggest that we work this out together and we will keep in close touch with you.

"Miss R will schedule another conference when the achievement scores come back.

"In the meantime feel free to contact us if you have any further concerns."

Mrs. J: "Thank you very much."

It is very unusual for a schoolman to get as involved in a parent concern as has been depicted in the J case.

It is instructive as we analyze this situation to realize that not only does Mrs. J have the usual adjustment problems that occur in moving from the city to the suburbs, but she also has individual problems with her daughter.

The change from city to suburbs requires a refocusing on many facets of living. The familiar landmarks, the friends and relatives, the services and often the pace is considerably different. Many times the city dweller is buying his first house and the frustrations in home ownership today are compounded by high interest rates, hidden costs, jerry-built construction, and increased status concerns over extras to the basic dwelling.

Add to this the mud and dust of the first year before a lawn is established and the need to develop new skills in home maintenance and one has additional frustrations in the adjustments from city to suburbs.

If a child has individual learning problems, the first year of adjustment to the new surroundings is unusually difficult.

Mrs. J has many of these problems and her concern about Susan's first-year teacher is brought out in her discussions with the principal and the school supervisor.

It would appear that her questioning of the school's grouping and marking system may be more the result of her daughter's having a less than sensitive teacher the first year than Susan's not being in the advanced class that her mother mentioned.

Hopefully, the fact that Mrs. J had two conferences early in the school year where the school leaders presented her with a considerable amount of school information plus giving her the all important opportunity to talk through her concerns, left her better informed and more ready to accept a different kind of school situation.

It is evident that the school leaders would have to reach the teacher involved so that she would be more able to understand the frustrations of the mother.

The teacher in the final analysis will make the difference in both the child's and the parent's attitude.

CHAPTER NINE

Different Types of Conferences

This chapter depicts six different types of conferences that teachers conduct. The reader would do well to refer to the guidelines to parent conferences as presented in the foreword. These directional aids plus the four approaches to parent conferences— the nonconfrontational, confrontational, indirect and direct—will help in further clarifying possible directions that one may take in each situation as presented.

The Casual Conference

The casual conference is rather common in suburbia. This is due to the fact that many teachers live and shop in the same town where they work.

The suburban teacher finds that she is approached by parents when she walks down the street, enters a bank or mails a letter.

The beauty parlor and the supermarket are the two major communication centers in suburbia. One may hear all the latest goings-on and rumors that abound in the community. A parent may travel through the detergents without incident only to be overwhelmed with school happenings at the cold-cut counter. It may take a parent three hours to traverse an "in" supermarket before she reaches the check-out counter. The beauty parlors are even more specialized and sensitive to stimulating agents. In so far as the beauty parlor has a clientele that sits and waits, it is a natural for local scuttlebutt.

The teacher cornered at the meat counter or grounded at the beauty parlor finds herself in an unusual position. The parent just wants to know how her Johnny is doing, what does she think about the teacher in the next room and is it true that the principal was brought on the carpet by a board member?

Unfortunately, much information leaks out into the community by way of these informal talks. Sometimes the teacher is not skilled enough to handle these situations and sometimes she views them as not part of the school job. After all, she may reason, I'm not on the job twenty-four hours a day.

The problem, however, is a little different when it comes to a child's parent who in seeing the teacher wants to take advantage of the meeting and asks about her child.

The teacher would do well to be brief and to limit her remarks by responding to the parent's questions in a matter-of-fact way. The teacher may want to set up an appointment for a future day. It would be well for the teacher not to go into depth on a problem, because this is neither the time nor the place. If anything this may lessen the professional importance of the teacher's role in the eyes of the parent. When a casual conference occurs, with concerns, it may give the teacher a firsthand idea of what to look for when a professional conference occurs.

The regular P.T.A. night is also a time when parents approach teachers on how their children are doing. This is a natural thing, and although most principals tell parents that P.T.A. nights are set aside for other things, parents and sometimes teachers seek each other out to talk about the child.

It is suggested that when this happens this be treated as a casual conference and any in-depth concerns be relegated to a conference by appointment.

Most teachers have experienced the parent with an urgent concern who intercepts the teacher as she enters the school building. These happenings should also be brief and matter of fact, and an appointment set up for a later conference.

The teacher may look upon the casual conference as a normal, social relationship pattern when it occurs outside the school, being careful not to get involved in a professional meeting at that time.

The Telephone Conference

The telephone conference may be initiated by the parent or by the teacher.

When the parent calls the teacher, it may be to impart some information such as, "I'm taking Barry to visit relatives for a week and I'd like some school work for him to do."

The call, however, may be made out of a parent's desperation. Sometimes the parent picks up misinformation at the supermarket and builds up concerns. The next-door neighbor's boy supposedly brought in cigarettes to school or the parent heard a rumor that the school was going to be integrated.

Calls of this sort can be handled simply by asking the parent to call the principal. The teacher would do well to alert the principal to the call so that he may be ready if any additional information is needed.

The angry parent call is generally in the form of a tirade. Here the parent is not visibly seen by the teacher, and I have found that an angry parent may be more abusive over the phone than when sitting with the teacher. There are times when the teacher has punished the child for a wrongdoing, when two children have had a fight on the playground, or when a teacher has said something to the child in class, that the teacher may not have seen as a major concern but is either magnified by the child when he gets home or is telescoped by an anxious parent.

These kinds of phone calls are most difficult because many parents will talk in a rapid-fire way which cannot be interpreted as a two-way conversation. I have had teachers who just hang on the other end of the receiver and wait for the talk to end after unsuccessfully trying to get a word in edgewise.

The teacher would do well to thank the parent for calling and arrange for a professional conference.

The teacher may have difficulty getting off the phone and she may remind the parent that she has another commitment to attend to.

Some teachers take insurance out against these kinds of calls by calling the parent if they anticipate a concern. Some teachers have their husbands answer the phone and take the message.

When a teacher calls a parent it is well for the call to be courteous, informative and brief. The teacher should plan what she wants to say, how to say it and why she is making the call.

Most parents are pleased when the teacher takes the time to call if their child is having trouble with school work or difficulty with another student in the class.

Here again the teacher should be aware that the child is an extension of the parent and that a scolding of the child is usually interpreted as reflecting on the parent. Too often the teacher fails to see the child as an alterego of the parent and in turn the parent himself feels reprimanded.

The Home Conference

The home conference was much more important with teachers when the school population was less urban. I suspect that today's changes in living with the emphasis upon a full calendar of after-school activities for teachers has minimized the home conference. The teacher today sees the professional day as a nine to three span and after-school activities become an extension of the professional commitment.

There are some teachers in suburbia who still make home visits and it is to these professionals that I speak. The home conference places the teacher in the position of guest of the parent. The teacher would do well to have clearly in mind the purpose of the meeting so that the conference will move along without awkward lapses in conversation. Thorough preparation and the techniques used in any good conference are in order for a home conference.

The advantage of a home visit is that the teacher has an opportunity to see the home situation and in this way gain insights into the child's background. All too often the teacher forgets that when a child comes to school he brings with him all his home experiences, which include his parents, brothers, sisters, friends, hobbies and pets.

The home visit is especially appropriate when the child has been absent for some time. Most school systems provide a home tutor. The classroom teacher by working closely with the tutor may coordinate the child's work and talk to the parent about the student's progress.

The parent may feel uncomfortable if the furniture and the surroundings are shabby and unattractive. The parent may also be condescending and try to overwhelm the teacher with the material splendor of her home.

I have experienced both situations and the best approach is to be completely professional.

The teacher is at the parent's home as an educational practitioner who has a service to render. Whether the teacher has coffee served from a chipped cup or from contemporary porcelain her manner should remain the same.

The Child-Parent Conference

The child-parent conference is one where either the teacher or the parent has the student present.

Some parents insist that their child be present at the conference so that the teacher may give support to the parent. This is sometimes the case in suburbia where the parent confuses her role as an adult with the student's role as a child. Strange as this may seem to some, the parent may find it difficult to discipline the child. The teacher then acts in a supportive role by talking first alone with the parent and then calling in the child for a three-way conference. When this occurs it would be well for the teacher to keep in touch with the parent so that a consistency in discipline and orientation may be accomplished.

The parent may want the child present at the conference to weigh his word against the teacher's. There are some parents who accept what their child says without question and during this kind of a conference equate the teacher's word with the student's. This also is an example of a confusion in role identification.

A relationship of this sort should be communicated to the principal who would want to take an active part in the total concern.

There are some parents who sincerely believe that children should be included in a parent-teacher conference so that the child may more fully understand what is happening. If this be the case, the teacher may want to meet with the child before the three-way conference so that the student may present some of his work to both adults and talk about the results. The teacher may participate with the child in commenting on work papers and other materials. A positive beginning to show the student's strong work areas is a good procedure. An understanding of the student's limitations should be developed tactfully with the student participating where possible. A constructive conclusion with an agreement for future action is important.

The Child-Teacher Conference

The child-teacher conference is becoming the pattern in more and more classrooms today. The teacher finds that a one-to-one relationship with the student builds understanding, reduces student concerns and enables the student to relate to an adult in a personalized way that is becoming more rare in today's contemporary society.

The skilled teacher constantly is building relationships with her students. At a time of increasing institutionalization of the suburban child through early nursery and pre-nursery experiences, after-school cultural activities, day camp and overnight camp commitments and sometimes for a complete summer, the teacher helps to fill the need of the child to relate to another human being on a one-to-one basis.

This personalized approach further reduces tensions because the student is better prepared to explain to his parents what he is doing in school. He also knows that the teacher supports him.

The teacher finds that by reviewing the report card individually before it goes home, the student is better able to express the card's meaning to his parents. This part of the child-teacher conference deserves careful attention because so many misunderstandings develop when the report is received by the parent. Especially in suburbia where so much emphasis is placed on academic achievement, the child's understanding of the card and his ability to relate what the card actually means is so important.

The student may still receive one dollar from his parents for each A received, but hopefully he will have a broader understanding of what the educator is trying to accomplish.

The Conference by Appointment

The conference by appointment is the preferred type of conference. The appointment implies that this meeting is important enough to set time aside for it. The time should be ample so that both the teacher and the parent do not feel rushed. This also provides the teacher time to plan properly for the conference. Materials and information are gathered so that the conference will be meaningful to the parent. Comfortable adult-size seats away from the teacher's desk in a quiet room help set the stage for the meeting. Some teachers serve coffee or tea so that a degree of informality and friendliness is evident.

The conference is begun on a positive note. At this time some of the child's accomplishments are displayed. At this time also, the parent may talk about his concerns. The teacher maintains a professional approach throughout the conference. The teacher-counselor refrains from using pedagogical jargon and tries to explain new concepts and approaches in language that the parent may understand.

A skilled teacher allows the parent to explore different problems that are on his mind and then attempts to structure the meeting so that the parent may work out his own solutions to these problems when possible.

There may be several solutions to a problem and it is possible that by talking with the parent the teacher may realize that her own preconceived solution would not be the best answer for this parent and his child.

This kind of honest exploration of a problem is possible as the teacher sets the stage for a conference where a dialogue between parent and teacher occurs.

CHAPTER TEN

In The Lion's Den

The immediate problem of the young teacher just out of college is one of awareness. He arrives at the public school armed with a variety of education courses, youthful idealism and varied and sundry experiences culled from student teaching.

Most young teachers have selected elementary education as a career because they have a leaning toward working with young children. They are idealistic and want to do something for kids. They generally are either from a middle-class home or have been trained at college to accept middle-class values. These young people are not adult orientated in the same way as secretaries or nurses are, but they tend to feel and think as people do who see the child's world as a special place.

This special something which makes for a good teacher can also make the young teacher less aware of the world of the child's mother. The problems of child rearing, household management, spouse keeping and suburban doings are all part of that other world. Yet the young teacher must become aware of this other world and how it relates to the child if he is to be a successful parent counselor.

The Mature Woman

The mature woman who comes back to teaching after child rearing has a different kind of awareness problem. She may have had an earlier, less pertinent, orientation-training program. This program may have been geared to different problems and ones that are already twenty years old. The kinds of relationships that were stressed by teachers then may not have the same kind of relevancy in today's fast-moving society.

The emphasis in instruction today is upon the individualization of instruction emphasizing the uniqueness of learning styles. The stress placed on relevancy especially as it relates to the intermediate student is one that the new teacher feels more deeply than his mature counterpart.

While the returnee gropes for educational understandings of twenty years ago, the new emphasis placed on modern math, individualized reading and programmed learning overshadows all else.

Probably the most difficult adjustment for the mature mother re-entering the school's orbit is the change in relationships between student and teacher. This change is felt mostly in the informal give and take in a classroom situation. Students are more prone to express themselves vocally than in the past. Although teachers are still "in charge of the classroom," the amount of student participation far exceeds anything seen in the past twenty years.

Student dress, attitude, vocabulary, ideas and recreational habits have so permeated the mass culture that a "think young" philosophy is widespread in the land today.

The alert teacher, whether a neophyte or a mature veteran, takes into account these cultural changes and adjusts his teaching style to them. Probably at no other time have young people been so bombarded by the mass media, and the good teacher takes advantage of the wealth of material that abounds to stimulate and structure learning.

The maturity of the teacher as a mother and as a wife helps her better understand children, especially if she is an active community member. This very important maturity factor pays dividends as she relates to other mothers whose children are in her care. It is not unusual to hear a mother state that her child's teacher is not one of those young things but has her own teen-age children.

We therefore have young teachers just out of college who may be loaded with enthusiasm and idealism, and also be quite unaware of the ways of the world while at the same time we have the mature mother coming back into teaching either to help put a child through college or for something to do with her time. She generally has many life experiences as a community member, mother and wife. These generalizations hold true; however, individual differences are to be considered and in the final analysis, age is not the best criteria in judging a potential teacher. Sometimes experiences in themselves are not that telling; the maturity of the individual is a better standard of judgment.

Some principals ask new teachers or teacher candidates certain questions such as what would you do if . . . Some principals simply rely on how well a potential teacher talks and dresses. Whether there are any factors that can be used to determine the maturity of a candidate other than a series of psychological tests is open to question.

The principal begins to build awareness in the new teacher the very first time he meets him. As he seeks understandings, he evaluates his readiness to work with the children and the parents of the school community. He consciously and unconsciously makes value judgments as to where and how the new teacher can best work. He visualizes approaches that he will use as they meet the job dimensions.

The In-Service Program

An in-service program begins that first summer before school when the principal asks the teacher to spend either a morning session or an afternoon one with him. When the teacher arrives, the principal has a packet of material ready which consists of basic manuals, teacher handbooks, school-district data and special notices and materials pertinent to his job assignment. The two-hour session may be viewed as an exploratory one where both the principal and the teacher discuss school philosophy, relationships with adults and students, and other immediate concerns of either the teacher or the principal. This initial dialogue enables the principal to set the stage and to clarify misunderstandings, especially as they concern relationships.

Witness the young teacher who believes that children should listen and not be heard; that children should show respect for him, the teacher, and dutifully raise their hands and take turns to speak;

and that they should respect each other as fellow human beings and not destroy each other's school property. How the principal responds to these ideas as he separates fact from fiction and begins to develop an awareness in this new teacher will largely determine the success or the failure of the first year's teaching experience.

As the principal walks the new teacher about the building showing him the lunchroom, the gymnasium, the library and the playground the principal answers his questions and thinks about the next in-service session.

In early September, prior to the opening of school, the P.T.A. president and the school principal send each new teacher an invitation to a luncheon orientation meeting. At this time, the new teachers are welcomed by the president of the P.T.A. and are introduced to the executive board members of the P.T.A. who act as hosts. The principal spends the rest of this session in presenting material not already given out and conducts a question and answer period. Many concerns are taken care of at this session where new teachers sometimes are more prone to speak out when with other neophytes than when alone with the principal. Needless to say, by this time the P.T.A. board members have left, leaving the principal with his new teachers. Special area personnel such as the school librarian and the psychologist may take advantage of this opportunity to brief new teachers about their service and school facilities. At this meeting new teachers should have an opportunity to develop lesson plans for the first week and to present them to the principal who will review them and comment before school begins. Some schools have a supervisor demonstrate register keeping, first-day procedures, schedules and other concerns at this time.

The total faculty meeting prior to the first day of school presents the principal with an opportunity to introduce the new teachers to the staff. Some schools initiate a buddy system where an experienced teacher takes a new teacher under his wing. Other schools have grade-level chairmen or team chairmen who take on this responsibility. Whatever way this is done, it is wise to have a specific veteran teacher responsible for looking after each new teacher. Generally, a brief meeting of new teachers after the first faculty meeting is helpful to answer any final concerns and to distribute any last-minute material or ideas.

After the first day of school, the principal calls a brief meeting of the new teachers to recap the day's events and to find out how he may help. Generally, there are lists of supplies teachers want that they did not find in their closets. Some teachers ask for information about a child or a specific procedure. This first day's recap is sometimes repeated on the second day by the principal and often, as he makes his rounds, he will drop into the new teacher's room to see if there is anything immediate that he can do during the first week.

Weekly meetings should be established immediately with new teachers. These meetings should be on a set day coinciding with the faculty meeting day. If Monday afternoon once per month is the faculty day, then every Monday should be set aside for a new teachers' meeting. In this way three Mondays of the month, new teachers can meet together and on the fourth Monday, they will have the benefit of the regular faculty meeting. New teachers' meetings should not be left to chance but should be carefully planned with prior agendas. Some principals poll their new teachers and find out what their needs are. In this way, meetings become more pertinent. Generally, the following areas are valuable for new teachers' meetings: discipline, curriculum problems in specific areas, register keeping, report cards, parent conferences, school rules and regulations, safety on the playground and supply ordering. Some schools have occasional open-ended meetings where new teachers can "let down their hair" and really talk out problems. Some principals use prepared tapes on curriculum matters to help stimulate discussion. Whatever the method used, new teachers should be encouraged to talk out their problems and not feel as though they are being evaluated by their principals at these meetings.

Part of a worthwhile in-service program includes careful reviewing of weekly lesson plans by the principal and the awareness that the principal has an open-door policy for any kind of problem that may develop whether it is school related or not.

The principal is not only available for difficult parent-teacher conferences, but he actively encourages new teachers to request his presence at some conferences. This activity not only enables him to be supportive of the teacher but it also presents the principal with an opportunity to teach the new staff member through his presence, ways of working with a parent. An alert teacher readily picks up cues from the principal on what and how to say difficult things.

Visitations, within the building and also to other school districts are a fruitful way to learn. The principal actively plans these activities keeping in mind the specific needs of the teacher and the classroom that can be visited with the maximum amounts of learning. A follow-up session carefully structured by the principal for visitations as well as other kinds of activities makes the difference not only in what the teacher gets out of the activity but also in the attitude that the new teacher develops toward his professional responsibility.

The Image of the New Teacher

The principal can do much to enhance the image of the new teacher in the eyes of the parents. Newspaper coverage of school openings should present background data on teachers new to the district. Occasionally, a school system having access to a radio station interviews new teachers.

During the course of the school year, the principal should bring to light unusual skills and experiences of the new teachers. These may be highlighted through P.T.A. programs, school projects and newspaper publicity.

The principal's enthusiasm for new teachers especially as he talks to parents about the fresh, creative ideas that new people bring to a school system goes far in allaying parent fears about their children having inexperienced teachers.

A good training program for the new teacher helps; however, some teachers have the ability to relate to parents while some teachers do not. The socially aware teacher senses parent concerns and knows how to put the parent at ease, to say just enough and to accept criticism without being defensive or hostile. Other teachers take offense easily, become aggressive and quickly get their backs up.

There are some excellent teachers who do a marvelous job with children but who often cannot achieve the same rapport with parents. When this happens a principal should gently encourage the teacher to see the parent as someone who needs more patience, and he should try to be present at the more difficult conferences.

There are suburban communities where some of these child-centered teachers will not wish to stay, especially if they are called upon to play a greater role in parent activities.

The Role of the Principal

The principal is the key person not only in the entire training program for the new teacher but especially in structuring attitudes on the part of the parent towards the staff. He sets the tone with parents in accepting and appreciating new teachers. He is supportive when the teacher finds himself in difficulties with a parent. He is quick to put down rumors which abound in every suburban community, all the while constantly building a positive image of the school staff.

Morale is one of the most difficult things to define, yet it is immediately perceived among staff members.

The principal can work for many months in building up good staff relationships, yet by making a simple blunder, he can destroy a great deal in a short time.

Therefore, the principal's task is one of always working with teachers and parents so that they can see the value of their partnership in working for children.

Often the importance of the student is overlooked when discussing the training of the new teacher. Yet acceptance by the student body largely determines the success of the new teacher. Here the established staff in working with children to develop a respect for teachers whether they be newcomers or veterans is very important.

When students are permitted to abuse school facilities and their fellow students, they in turn will show a lack of respect for the teacher.

CHAPTER ELEVEN

The Teacher as

Parent Counselor

As I worked with teachers, we developed a parent-teacher conference form which provided a place to elaborate on the conference's basis and outcome. We also included a place for what we called the "climate of the conference." It was our intention to think through the feeling tones of the conference so that we all would become more sensitive to the subtleties of the parent-teacher relationship.

I developed a parent-teacher conference worksheet so that as conference forms were sent to me I could identify them with one of the four approaches used.

The parent-teacher conference worksheets included in this chapter have a very brief evaluation added in order to clarify the author's interpretation of the conference.

A Parent Problem in Social Awareness

Case no. 781H (direct)

Mr. and Mrs. H view school as a place where students learn reading, writing and arithmetic and where the teacher acts as an imparter of knowledge. The school is seen as an institution where a person goes to pick up certain needed marketable skills. The school is a necessary interlude in a person's life to be accepted for what it is, an imparter of skills and knowledge.

92

PARENT-TEACHER CONFERENCE WORKSHEET

Case No. 781H

Approach	Basis of Discussion	Climate of the Conference	Outcome of the Conference
The Direct Approach "Telling-imparting one"	"Kenneth is not working anywhere near his potential."	"Mrs. H. finally accepted the fact that there is a problem."	"Mrs. H wanted me to speak to her husband."
	"He does very little in school."	"She rejected the suggestion that the principal speak to her son."	"Mr. H called me in the evening. He seemed primarily concerned with Kenneth's work habits rather than his behavior toward other children."
"highly structured"	"He does not get along well with the other children in the class."	"She had nothing to say except that her husband would know what to do."	"I suggested that I could write about Kenneth's school progress every week."
"Parent is a passive member of the conference"	"Since school has begun he has not done a homework assignment."	"Mrs. H. ridiculed my suggestion that Kenneth join the Boy Scouts."	"These reports will go home and be signed by Mr. H."

Mr. and Mrs. H place little emphasis upon Kenneth's social development and even look upon the school's attempt to discipline the child as an infringement of their rights and responsibilities as parents.

This viewpoint is partly due to the fact that Mr. H is a highly successful free-lance writer who believes in setting his own standards. He objects to working for someone else and sees society as an inhibiting force that stifles creativity.

Mrs. H calls herself a bohemian and she looks down upon the regularized suburban patterns of dinner parties, coffee klatches and swim-club commitments.

Her children call her by her first name and she freely uses profanity as a way of expressing herself.

She considers herself a freethinker and encourages her children to speak their minds.

The teacher felt constantly frustrated by the parents deemphasizing social goals and viewing the adjustment to others as secondary to academic learning.

The desire of the teacher to give Kenneth a social outlet by having him join the Boy Scouts and the negative reaction to this suggestion on the part of the mother highlights the different orientation of the two women.

The direct approach of the teacher in suggesting a weekly progress report is helpful in that it permits the teacher to approach the parent through an academic channel.

The teacher knows that she must be firm and direct with Mr. and Mrs. H because they are not ready to talk through their son's antisocial behavior.

The teacher is also aware that when parents rebel against the accepted folkways of a community, their children will reflect this attitude and that until the parents can be reached little will be done with the children.

A First-Year Teacher Handles an Explosive Situation

Case no. 524A (indirect)

Mr. A, an intense, anxious parent, had an opportunity to "chew

PARENT-TEACHER CONFERENCE WORKSHEET

Case No. 524A

Approach	Basis of Discussion	Climate of the Conference	Outcome of the Conference
The Indirect Method "The teacher acts as a sounding board for the parent's concerns." "Cathartic-type conferences" "A verbal discharge"	"Mr. A complained of the teacher's giving his child excessive homework, oppressive assignments, impossible questions, and ridiculous tasks.'" "Mr. A questioned the reading program stating that too much money was spent on supplementary books and material while too little was spent on teacher's salaries."	"Mr. A showed considerable emotion as he harangued the teacher for 'penalizing the entire class for some students talking out.' He stated that his child is 'going to a deprived school due to the fact that there has been a change in teacher personnel in his child's class.'"	"Mr. A appeared more relaxed after the initial tirade was over. He stated that now he felt better. He laughed and said, 'Yes, I feel better, we must get together some-time.'"

out" a first-year teacher in a conference which was carried on as a parent monologue.

It is unusual for a father alone to attend a parent-teacher conference and when this happens the teacher would do well to look for other concerns.

In this case the mother had "steamed up" the father sufficiently so that he decided to face the teacher alone.

The initial concern that Mr. A brought to the conference is unfortunately a common mistake of the new teacher. The class misbehaved and the teacher rather than reprimanding only those guilty punished the entire class by having everybody write five hundred times, "I must be good in school." Mr. A's daughter happened to be one of the innocent children in the class.

The teacher knew that Mr. A was an explosive person. The parent had a reputation of "sounding off" about the schools and of chastising individual teachers at board of education meetings.

The teacher fortunately checked with the principal and, having reevaluated the situation, realized his error and decided to allow the parent to talk out his concern. The teacher realized that if Mr. A spoke long and loud enough he would feel better.

The teacher was able to maintain his composure during the conference. He assumed the indirect method of conferencing where he acted as a sounding board for the parent's concern.

An alternative to this method could very well have been a confrontation. It is natural for a teacher to get his dander up and to strike back. When a parent "comes on hard" the teacher could act in a similar fashion and as sparks fly things are usually said that cannot be taken back.

Many a parent's complaint to a board of education member is the result of a poorly handled conference. This kind of head-on collision is quite costly in time and energy to the schoolman and the work involved is hardly worth it.

An Unnecessary Kindergarten Concern

Case no. 821L (confrontational)

Mrs. L, a kindergarten parent, had taken Donald to a reading clinic to be tested before this parent-teacher conference. The school

PARENT-TEACHER CONFERENCE WORKSHEET

Case No. 821L

Approach	Basis of Discussion	Climate of the Conference	Outcome of the Conference
Confrontational "A conflict situation is developed" "A head-on struggle" "a coolness in relationships"	"I tried to discuss with Mrs. L, Donald's behavior at home, his relationship to his older sister, his short attention span, and his excessive aggressiveness." "Mrs. L did not seem to hear anything that was said other than about his aggressiveness. Mrs. L attributed this to the fact that the children he used to play with are a few months older than Donald and are now in the first grade. He is no longer accepted by this group and he is considered to be 'a baby.' The mother feels that we both have to help him to make friends and this will solve the social problem."	"Mrs. L feels that his speech is inconsistent because I do not give him enough time to speak and therefore he must get everything in while he has the chance." "I did not discuss some of the other things in my anecdotal records because the mother was unreceptive and she ignored so many things I mentioned that I got the feeling that she would not listen to anything else."	"Mrs. L requested that she meet with the principal because she feels that I don't understand Donald."

authorities had not been notified by the clinic of the testing and the teacher was completely surprised when the mother accused her of not adequately instructing her child.

Mrs. L came to the conference most concerned about the instructional program, armed with I.Q. data and related reading scores that she had received from the private reading clinic.

Mrs. L talked incessantly during the conference and the few times that the teacher spoke, the parent either ignored her or stated that she wanted to see the principal.

This conference really backfired. The parent spent a number of lengthy conferences with the principal who in turn attempted to unravel the problem by meeting with the kindergarten teacher and communicating with the private reading clinic.

Actually, the mother's fears started with the child's obvious immaturity and were inadvertently accentuated by the teacher's handling of earlier conferences. The teacher, having noticed Donald's poor coordination and aggressive behavior, spoke to the mother about possible retardation. The mother in turn sought advice from a private clinic which reassured her that although the child was immature for his age, there was no noticeable retardation present.

The teacher would have done well to share her observations with the principal and set up either a three-way meeting with the mother or else chat informally with the mother about Donald's need for more social experiences.

The teacher obviously became very short with the parent and this further aggravated an already tense situation.

This is another example of the need of the teacher's being sensitive to parent concerns. Sometimes a word or a facial expression by the teacher may set off an already concerned parent.

Robert Read All the Reading Books

Case no. 324M (confrontational)

Mrs. M presents a common problem found in the parent-teacher conference, that of the teacher-turned-parent. In addition to Mrs. M's not knowing how to relate to the schools as a parent, she becomes arrogant and insinuates that the teacher doesn't know how to teach.

PARENT-TEACHER CONFERENCE WORKSHEET

Case No. 324M

Approach	Basis of Discussion	Climate of the Conference	Outcome of the Conference
Confrontational "A conflict situation is developed" "A head-on struggle" "A coolness in relationships"	"Robert's progress on the whole and his reading level. Mother who is a teacher put Robert through the reading series. Robert was tested by the school's reading teacher. He said Robert's sight vocabulary is very poor. He is on a primary level. The problem was where to place Robert since he had already read the district's reading series."	"The parents were *extremely arrogant.*" "Mrs. M wanted to know if Robert was tested properly— what tests were used, etc." "The supervisor was called in."	"Robert reads with the top group and receives individual instruction in another primer. The parents still did not seem pleased." "I don't know what more they wanted." "I feel that all they wanted was for me to say that Robert was an excellent reader." "I could not say that for he lacks many skills."

Unfortunately for her child, Mrs. M, in her intense desire to have Robert accelerate in school, has taken him through the school's primary basal reading series.

This is not uncommon in suburbia where parents will buy reading series for their children and teach them to read before they enter the first grade.

The teacher, a first-year professional, became flustered during the conference and words were exchanged with the parent. Fortunately, the elementary supervisor was able to stabilize the situation by meeting with the teacher and the parent and interpreting test scores.

Mrs. M was then better able to see Robert in relation to the other students in the room. The situation might have been more difficult if Robert were the only child reading in his class, but in suburbia this generally is not the case.

This case pinpoints the need continually to orientate parents to the way in which the reading program works and the necessity to have parents come in and talk over their concerns about their children's reading before these concerns overwhelm the parent.

The teacher's fumbling was partially due to her inexperience. However, it would have been better if she had asked the parent to meet with the elementary supervisor where reading scores could be reviewed by another professional.

The M conference will be reviewed later in this chapter and other alternative approaches will be suggested.

The Teacher-turned-parent

Case no. 489F (nonconfrontational)

Mrs. F recently moved here from the South. She is a very tense, exacting mother who constantly hovers over her son, William.

She has a very low estimate of her son's ability, and instead of buiding up his image she does things for him so that he doesn't have an opportunity to experience success brought about by his own efforts.

The teacher sensed that the mother was not to be met head-on but needed an opportunity to talk over her concerns and to be reassured of what she was doing for William. At the same time the

PARENT-TEACHER CONFERENCE WORKSHEET

Case No. 489F

Approach	Basis of Discussion	Climate of the Conference	Outcome of the Conference
Non-confrontational	"Mrs. F feels that William is the least successful of her children. Mother is concerned that children torment William at the bus stop."	"I conveyed the feeling to the mother that we should concentrate more on making William feel worthwhile and deemphasize the academic trend."	"Mother agreed also that William should see the school psychologist."
"Hostility is dissipated"			"If mother would let William develop on his own, this would be a step forward in his progress."
"shared concerns"	"I told mother that William can sit for hours and accomplish nothing, yet he thrives on praise when his work is well done."	"I suggested that William stay with me and not attend the reading clinic as he will become more confused."	
"accepting, non-threatening atmosphere"			
"structuring of the problem"	"He is a loner and does not mix too easily with the other boys."		
"follow-up meeting"			

teacher attempted to encourage Mrs. F to allow William to take responsibility for doing things around the house and to make mistakes without being castigated.

The teacher allayed Mrs. F's fears by giving her an opportunity to review test scores together. Telephone calls were endless and each afternoon Mrs. F stopped in to pick up William and to chat with the teacher.

The teacher soon learned not to touch off Mrs. F's alarm system, and she found it necessary to call her whenever certain notices went home. The teacher managed to get through the year with an explosive situation that never quite went off.

Mrs. F, an ex-school teacher presents the teacher-turned-parent problem. She confuses the role of the past teacher with the role of the present mother. She needs a great deal of guidance and reassurance.

It would have been very easy for the teacher to allow this situation to deteriorate into a confrontation. It did require an additional amount of perseverance on the part of the teacher because Mrs. F constantly referred to her own teaching "success" and methods that she used with children in improving their reading skills.

A Child Needs Affection

Case no. 520S (nonconfrontational)

Mrs. S, a very tense, compulsive mother, had an opportunity to express her concerns to the teacher. Mrs. S finds it very difficult to control Nancy and she is constantly embarrassed by the stories Nancy makes up about her. Some of the stories have sexual overtones, and when Mr. S is told of this he restricts Nancy to the house for the rest of the week.

The mother views the child as one who should be in a special class where the child's aggressive attitudes may be corrected.

There are some mothers who read into their children a number of physical and psychological problems. Many suburban parents seek out college courses and community workshops that specialize in psychological problems of the young.

It also becomes fashionable to solve all family problems by referring to some psychological theory.

PARENT-TEACHER CONFERENCE WORKSHEET

Case No. 520S

Approach	Basis of Discussions	Climate of the Conference	Outcome of the Conference
Non-confrontational	"Mrs. S is concerned because Nancy comes home from school very tense, explodes in the house and then goes outside and deliberately picks fights with the neighbor's children."	"I explained to mother that Nancy has a need to show affection to others, and although she has difficulty making girl friends she does display a degree of tenderness in taking care of the class hamster."	"I told the mother that Nancy is a very creative child who seeks out attention whenever possible."
"hostility is dissipated"			
"shared concerns"	"Mrs. S stated that Nancy makes up stories about her and tells the neighbors."	"At first the mother was afraid that Nancy would be bitten by the hamster, but later she agreed to allow her to continue with this project."	"She does have an overactive imagination and it is necessary to employ a degree of firmness in working with her so that she may relax and concentrate."
"accepting, non-threatening atmosphere"			
"structuring the problem"			
"follow-up meeting"			

After Mrs. S vented her fears of Nancy's being different, the teacher encouraged her to seek out the school psychologist.

It would be well if the teacher could show the parent that Nancy's display of affection for the hamster could be taken advantage of at home by giving her tasks to do where both mother and daughter work together on a shared responsibility.

Nancy's need for affection is obvious and it would be encouraging to think that possibly the school psychologist may enable mother and father to realize this.

It becomes evident that a skilled elementary teacher in suburbia is more than earning his keep. He not only must be proficient in teaching all areas of the curriculum but must be extremely skilled in working with a wide range of parents, some of whom are living in very tense situations.

The tension of the home spills over into the classroom and the teacher must be constantly alerted to early morning danger signals. These may appear when a child has experienced an early morning upset from mother and father fighting at the breakfast table. They become evident when a primary child must prepare his own breakfast and see himself off to the bus stop without praise or the reassurance of a parent present.

The Minority Child

Case no. 394T (nonconfrontational)

Mrs. T, being a member of a minority group, felt uncomfortable and only complained when the situation became unbearable. The other children in the school had teased her daughter, Maria, to the point where the child refused to eat lunch.

Fortunately, Maria's teacher was very sympathetic, and she hovered over her and attempted to be supportive wherever possible.

The teacher worked with Mrs. T and a common course of action was agreed upon, namely to constantly remind Maria of her worth as an individual. The teacher also helped Mrs. T to realize that changes will not occur overnight as these feelings that Maria has have been building up as a result of many negative experiences with other children.

The elementary supervisor began to work with Maria and an

PARENT-TEACHER CONFERENCE WORKSHEET

Case No. 394T

Approach

Non-confrontational

"hostility is dissipated"

"Shared concerns"

"accepting non-threatening atmosphere"

"structuring of the problem"

"follow-up meeting"

Basis of Discussion

"Mrs. T is *very upset* because children in the cafeteria and on the bus call Maria smelly and stupid. Maria *cannot* eat in school and has missed her bus intentionally."

"Maria has *very low self-esteem.* She will not believe it when I tell her that something is good that she has done. She likes school but thinks herself worthless. Mrs. T is aware of this and blames the last two years in school for Maria's attitude."

Climate of the Conference

"The climate of the conference was one of desperation. Mrs. T did not bring the problem to my attention before because she did not think it was the right thing to do. She knows that Maria can take no more! Mrs. T related that Maria is allowed to play with but one child in the development. The neighbors will not allow Maria in their houses because she is different."

"Maria is a very sweet child and will never fight back when the children say cruel things about her."

Outcome of the Conference

"Mrs. T and I both agreed that Maria must be continuously told of her worth. I told Mrs. T to speak with the supervisor because she was still emotionally upset. Mrs. T felt better and realized that a change in Maria will not occur overnight; it might take many years for Maria to feel that she is worth something as an individual."

attempt was made to help her become part of the library club. Membership in this school organization was sought by many students.

Unfortunately, suburbia's children become so homogeneous that they don't have an opportunity to mix with other children. The higher the income level of the parent, the more expensive the house and the less likelihood there is that people of other socio-economic levels will buy a house in the immediate area.

At one time the public schools were looked upon as the great democratization experience for all children. This melting-pot action in the upper-income suburbs is possible, however, only by integration through bussing, which although somewhat successful is costly and does set up an artificial social situation.

The middle school has been an interesting attempt by some communities to better meet the academic challenges in today's knowledge explosion. While the emphasis has been on the fact that our children mature physically and intellectually at an earlier age today, we should not lose sight of the possibility that a middle school may introduce our suburban youngsters to other children at an earlier age.

A Concern Between Mother and Daughter

Case no. 497Z (direct)

It is obvious that Mrs. Z has deep feelings about her daughter when she tells the teacher that "Julie is not getting enough of a challenge" and that "Julie has a very arrogant attitude about her ability."

It is also obvious that the teacher is not "tuned-in" to the parent's concern as she states, "Julie has never exhibited any superior attitude and so I was unaware that it existed."

It would appear that both women are trying to state their concerns about Julie and yet are communicating on different wave lengths.

The parent displays a concern about her daughter which speaks of a competition that is common between mother and daughter.

The teacher is not only missing the mother's concern, but she is highly defensive about the girl. The teacher states that, "I could

PARENT-TEACHER CONFERENCE WORKSHEET

Case No. 497Z

Approach	Basis of Discussion	Climate of the Conference	Outcome of the Conference
Direct "Telling-imparting one" "highly structured" "parent is a passive member of the conference"	"Although I had only good things to say about Julie's work, Mrs. Z was not satisfied. She feels that Julie is not getting enough of a challenge." "She states that Julie has a very arrogant attitude about her ability and she feels that this is not good." "Mrs. Z is sorry that Julie is a committee chairman because she feels that this gives Julie something else to feel superior about." "Mrs. Z wants Julie to be put in a class next year where she is not the best student."	"I explained to Mrs. Z that Julie is being instructed at her ability level in *all* subject areas regardless of what the other children in the class are doing. She does not appear to be bored in school nor does she find everything so terribly easy (especially math)." "Julie has never exhibited any superior attitude in school and so I was unaware it existed. Mrs. Z appreciated this fact and only wanted to inform me about this side of Julie's personality (which she says exists)."	"I could see Mrs. Z's point about Julie always having been the best student in the class, but I tried to convince her that Julie would be a good student regardless of the class she was in."

see Mrs. Z's point about Julie always having been the best student in the class, but I tried to convince her that Julie would be a good student regardless of the class she was in."

The school psychologist should be involved in this case conference to help the mother see through some of her obvious, negative feelings towards her daughter. Unfortunately, the school psychologist is brought into a conference only when the parent gives her permission.

This kind of hit or miss use of a highly skilled professional is unfortunate for it leaves to the classroom teacher the decision of whether or not the psychologist should be suggested to the parent.

The skill of the teacher in convincing the parent to utilize the psychologist varies with each teacher so that the utilization of this vital team member may rest upon many variable factors rather than upon a professional judgment.

I have presented these eight conferences just as I received them from the parent-teacher conference forms. These forms do not indicate the intensive work involved in preparing for a parent conference or the follow-up that may involve a team of professionals for many months.

Parents usually don't realize that thorough preparation for a parent conference may take hours of work and the twenty to thirty minutes involved in the conference is a concentrated effort on the part of the teacher in presenting and discussing informational data.

Likewise, the follow-up sessions may continue for the rest of the school year with many professionals involved. Meetings, phone calls to other teachers who have taught the student and record keeping are all behind-the-scenes activities that may go unnoticed by the parent.

The 524 A conference was successful partly due to the sensitivity of a beginning teacher. The indirect approach used worked well with a parent who had left teaching after he had been passed by when administrative promotions were given out. The bitterness of this experience accentuated an already turbulent personality and goaded him on to berate school people at every opportunity.

The question left unanswered is how will the teacher follow up his initial gain with the parent so that he may continue to work well with him.

Skilled teacher-counselors find that the more data they can accumulate about a parent-child situation before the conference, the more accurate are they in piecing together a truer picture of the problem. Experienced teachers find that it is more difficult to gather data on a highly mobile population than it was when parents moved less.

Mrs. Z of the 497 Z case would have responded better to an indirect approach than to a direct telling, imparting one. A parent who has deep feelings about her child should have an opportunity at school to talk about her concerns.

A skilled teacher would allow the mother to talk and then suggest additional professional help for the child. In this way the mother would not feel that the teacher is being defensive about Julie or siding with the child against her but is supportive of the parent's concern.

Once a psychologist begins to work with the child, the parent becomes an active part of the process and is brought into therapy.

Experienced teachers sense which parent-conference approach to use as they work directly with the parent. Some teachers favor one approach over another, but most skilled teachers pick up cues as they enter the dialogue. Changes are sometimes made at that time.

Although I favor the nonconfrontational method, there are times when it is less than effective and the 324 M case is one example where a direct approach was needed.

A teacher could spend a great deal of time structuring a situation after allowing the parent to talk out her concerns. In the case of Mrs. M, a skilled teacher would have set the record straight by presenting in a positive way not only where the child stands in relation to his classmates but how the mother, as a teacher, should view the school.

In the case of the inexperienced teacher, as mentioned earlier, she would rely on the elementary supervisor to present in a matter-of-fact manner what the mother should, as well as should not, do with her son's school involvement.

Sometimes a parent is helped more by the teacher's coming to the point immediately and clearing the air. This would be the case with Mrs. M. The degree of skill that a teacher brings to the conference will largely determine the success of this method. Here again, the experienced teacher senses that this is the way to work with Mrs. M.

The approach that Mrs. L of Case 821 used in going to a private clinic to allay her fears about her kindergarten child is becoming all too common in the metropolitan area.

She may have gone to a private psychologist or neurologist and received similar data. Unfortunately, private professionals sometimes feel that they must give their clients professional data in return for money paid. As a result the schools spend many hours unraveling misunderstood and isolated data. It is not unusual for an aggressive parent to ask the private professional to write a letter to the school requesting that the child's teacher be changed or that he be placed in an advanced section.

The attiutde of the private reading clinic in the 821 L case is not unusual. When the principal contacted the clinic he was told that Mr. and Mrs. L were too intense with their child and that they should try to become more relaxed. When the principal asked whether they discussed this with the parents, the answer he received was that the parents were not told this but they were requested to talk with their child's teacher about his school's reading program.

Who takes the responsibility for telling the parent that he is pressuring the child?

What control if any should the public schools have on the private professional as he works with and directly affects public school children?

CHAPTER TWELVE

P.T.A.—Cooperative Partnership

or Destructive Force?

An understanding of parent-teacher relationships must take into account the P.T.A. This organization of parents and teachers may be as different as day and night depending on the local setting. A rural P.T.A. is generally passive and it limits its activities to cake sales, occasional guest speakers and being a cooperative arm of the school principal. A P.T.A. in a settled suburban or urban area may be active and involve itself in controversial, internal school affairs in relation to the intensity of the problems inherent in the local school system. The P.T.A.'s of burgeoning, tax-burdened suburbia are indeed active organizations.

Parents join P.T.A. for a variety of reasons. In the growing suburbs this is the thing to do. Active P.T.A.'ers work with the school authorities through flyers, local radio announcements and newspaper publicity. One P.T.A. president suggested that P.T.A. dues be added to the school tax bill. While most parents join P.T.A. as a matter of being part of suburbia, some join because they believe that they can effect change. The motivation for these activist parents varies. The mother who really is frustrated in not having put her college education to use and who now is changing diapers looks for an opportunity to express her educational views. The parent with a real conviction that education is too soft, not phonetically orientated, not basic or not socially aware, finds a ready place in the P.T.A. The neurotic parent who needs an outlet and is the pile driver on church committees, civic organizations and local political groups finds the P.T.A. a likely arena to express herself. Dominant, submissive, well-informed, biased and just plain housewives are all part of the P.T.A. that the principal and his professional staff work with everyday of the school year.

The Principal in a P.T.A. Setting

The role of the building principal in such a setting becomes crucial not only to his building but also to the school district. One situation comes to mind where a rather naïve principal, believing himself to be democratic, allowed an activist group of parents to capture both the executive board of the P.T.A. and the total parent organization. This vocal group started with a request to act as an advisory board to the principal. He readily agreed seeing this as an opportunity to have parent participation. The principal had learned this concept at the university where he took his master's degree in school administration. The professor, having been too long removed from the principal's hot seat, theorized democratic administration without the depth of practical awareness.

The building principal was soon led down the garden path by the activist parents. He first agreed to a change in the sex education program and then to having parents evaluate teachers for tenure. The principal had some misgivings about parent evaluations of teachers, but he rationalized this approach by saying that the children really belonged to the parents. Things soon got out of hand and the parent group began making demands on the local board of education to establish a district-wide parent evaluation committee for all teachers and administrators. Fortunately, a firm superintendent supported by a rational board of education was able to bring the situation to a halt. The harm that an unaware principal allowed in this case was felt for many years in the school system.

The principal and his teacher advisors to the P.T.A. should work directly with the P.T.A. executive board. The importance of an executive board should never be minimized. Parents generally are asked to become executive board members by the president through a phone call. On occasion a parent will seek out a place on the executive board. Whatever the case, preplanning and understanding on the part of the president and the principal determine whether the P.T.A. will be a positive force or a destructive one.

The principal should carefully structure procedures and understandings with the P.T.A. president so that the role of a supporting parent organization and the role of the professional educator are clearly understood. The P.T.A. national and state literature are clear in stating that P.T.A. is a partnership working with the schools, and in no way is the organization to be viewed as one that would usurp the professional role of the schoolman. Interference in school administration is strongly frowned upon.

The principal as he structures the role of the professional in partnership with the parent outlines practices and procedures that will be helpful to the P.T.A. president as she functions both as the president and as the chairman of the P.T.A. executive board.

Firstly, the principal should through numerous dialogues with the president explore the mutual concern that parent and teacher have for children, stressing the professional role of the teacher. As a professional educator, the teacher uses sound judgment, professional know-how and is specially trained and certified for his teaching assignment. He knows that there are school procedures to follow when difficulties with a student or a parent arise and he works directly with the building principal. The parent as an alert citizen-partner in the educational enterprise knows that concerns first are presented to the classroom teacher and only when an impasse is reached does she present the problem to the principal. She is aware that it is improper to contact a board member or the superintendent, for the principal is the responsible authority in the building.

Secondly, an attitudinal approach toward people on all levels cooperating and communicating with each other is needed. The P.T.A. president should have an opportunity to talk through concerns she may have as a parent. The way the principal handles her fears, concerns and aspirations will largely determine how successful the parent-principal cooperative endeavor will be.

I have known principals who publicly call their P.T.A. presidents their "vice principals" and do not make a move without first clearing matters through them. I am also aware that some principals make decisions on parent meetings, boundary-line changes (when it is their jurisdiction), and pupil transfer from one school to another without considering, to say nothing of calling, the P.T.A. president.

A principal would do well to inform and consult his P.T.A. president when pupil boundary changes and other "sticky" issues develop. A proper understanding of the relative roles played by parent and teacher and a sound attitude toward mutual respect go very far when the chips are down.

The principal should have an opportunity to consult with the P.T.A. president when executive board members are selected. This in no way implies a control system but a two way communication which is all too lacking in many suburban schools. Scuttlebutt travels so fast in the suburbs that even with the best of relationships, misunderstandings commonly occur. I would go so far as to say that in each principal's life there are three women: his wife, his secretary and his P.T.A. president.

The executive board meeting is so important that if a principal must on occasion miss a meeting he should have some other professional there in his place. Many school districts now have teacher representatives on the local P.T.A. executive board. It is at the executive board that the principal often receives firsthand information about concerns in the neighborhood because board members are not only active in their local school units but in many other local activities. The principal makes his presence felt if a member decides to push for some vested interest such as a fund drive for an organization or for some unusual curriculum concern. The principal as the representative of the schools also clarifies concerns and misinformation. He presents information and attitudes that help to keep the school on an even keel.

The posture that the principal takes, especially in an emergency, is critical. The unsure parent is quick to detect an uncertain principal or a deep concern. As the principal projects confidence in the school enterprise, executive board parents likewise tend to develop a positive attitude.

Some principals take the last ten minutes of every executive board meeting to bring parents up to date with goings-on in the school. These principals reason that executive board parents, being the spark plugs of the organization, need to be well informed.

Often, special area personnel, a psychologist or a reading special-
ist, is brought in to further inform and to orientate.

Pitfalls in a School Program

There are a number of pitfalls which may hurt a school program
and which a principal may unwittingly encourage. The principal
who permitted a citizen's group to evaluate teachers and to advise
him on school programs is one glaring example. The principal
must realize that he is dealing with very complex situations today.
Many unmet needs and concerns are found in some parents and
often at a citizen's meeting what is really meant is left unsaid. The
principal has to translate words, attitudes and facial expressions
into a reasonably correct statement. If he takes what is said at face
value, he will find himself in a confusing and misunderstood situation.

A parent poked her head into the principal's office and blurted
out "this will just take a minute" and proceeded to thrust herself
into the office. The principal sighed and said to himself, "This will
just take a minute—famous last words." At this point the parent
opened up with a diatribe that shook the rafters. After ten minutes
of rapid-fire accusations, which ranged from the need for law and
order in the school to a concern about school secretaries taking a
coffee break, the mother broke down and said that she was deathly
frightened about a demonstration at the high school where she had
a son. The principal fortunately was able to maintain his composure,
all the while sensing that something else was bothering the parent.
If he took each one of her accusations at face value and attempted
to answer them, he would not only engage the parent in a fruitless
dialogue but would open up other areas that were better left un-
discussed.

How does a principal develop this kind of know-how? There are
no easy answers, but certainly the ability to listen to a parent and
to pick up concerns helps. When a principal is tuned-in to his community and especially has a close communication system with his
executive board he at least has a fighting chance.

The principal who procrastinates either out of fear or lack of
skill may cause damage to his school. A teacher asked for a decision

on how to handle holiday parties. Some teachers called these parties winter parties, others Christmas parties. Some teachers brought in Christmas trees, others simply had grab bags. Some classes sang Christmas carols, others sang songs about sleigh bells. The principal promised teachers that he would look into their concern and issue a memo that would clarify the holiday situation. He did not act on their concerns. One teacher dressed up as Santa Claus and visited several primary classes, wishing children a Merry Christmas. The next day when a board of education member called the principal and stated that several parents called him and complained that religion had entered the schools, the principal had no answer.

An unusual situation developed when a high-powered P.T.A. member voiced her concern about her child's class placement. The mother stated that the teacher was in direct conflict with her child. The principal listened and stated that if it would help, he would change the child's class. The parent suggested which teacher she wanted for her child. The principal knowing that the mother was a real pile driver readily agreed. Word got around the community and the principal was bombarded by similar requests. He went to the superintendent for help; however, the damage was done. Here is a case where the principal not only gave in to the demands of a vocal parent but by doing so opened the door for many other request problems.

In suburbia it is not unknown for parents to request teacher changes. Some parents ask for special privileges for their children. Some ask that their child take a later bus on certain days of the week because the mother is out Monday, Wednesday and Friday afternoons, or to check to see that the child is reminded on Tuesdays and Thursdays to go through the garage as the front door is locked.

The principal may play the role of arbitrator, conciliator and mediator all in a day's time. He is constantly alert to staying out of family fights and neigborhood law suits. His role is one where he clearly draws the line between the school's responsibility for the child when the student is on school grounds and the parent's responsibility for the child when off school grounds. Most parents understand this, yet there is a constant attempt in suburbia to draw the principal into conflicts which occur among parents and children outside the school.

The suburban principal today, more than at any other time, is involved as an active member of all P.T.A. functions. He realizes the need to project a positive image of the school. This is not a way of fooling the public but reveals a real understanding that people need the security and the reassurance that the schools know where they are going. The principal knows that parent involvement not only brings support but also perimts him to work closely with parents and help them better understand their child and the school's program.

One principal started a series of weekly, parent education forums. These grew out of a real need felt by parents and communicated to the principal. A committee of parents led by the principal established a format where school-district professionals as well as outside speakers came into the school to talk on various subjects. The topics dealt with child behavior, teen attitudes, today's changing values and curriculum innovations. Many of the active, interested parents of the school district had a chance to participate and to get a better understanding of current problems. The principal built support for his school district as well as helped to answer some real concerns that some parents had, thereby avoiding possible future conflicts.

The P.T.A. is a natural vehicle in developing a cooperative partnership between home and school. This partnership is achieved not by talking through goals, although that is important, but by careful planning and actually doing the kind of job that is needed on a day-by-day basis. The principal and the P.T.A. president work to obtain the confidence of the parent group and to build faith in their leadership so that when mistakes are made or when inevitable difficulties arise, there will be a strong foundation of community support for school policy.

A case in point is one where a junior high school principal was accused by one of his custodians of physically assaulting him in the halls. The papers made much of this situation, and while the principal had already been cleared of these charges by the board of education, the problem of parent credibility was a real one. The principal was able to fall back on his past performance in working with people and in the relationships he had developed with parents and teachers. People knew that he had patiently worked through many "sticky" parent problems in the past.

It is obvious that the principal today is in the open arena of community action. He is becoming more skilled in comunications, although he was not trained to any great extent in the art of communicating to adults. I suspect that most college professors are not tuned-in to the local school situation and the influence of the few that are is hardly felt. While the principal readjusts to a new role in the community and in the schools he realizes the vast potential of the P.T.A. and he works to establish a positive linkage to the parent.

Some principals conduct weekly coffee klatches held during the school day. These meetings may introduce a new program, help clarify existing programs and enable parents to discuss their concerns with the principal.

A new innovation of the school coffee klatch is having one each week in a parent's home. This type of informal setting works well in bringing in neighborhood parents. In such a home environment, the principal has an opportunity to further clarify programs and approaches used in his school.

It is through the P.T.A. and especially through the president and the executive board that a better understanding of the parent-teacher relationship is developed. The role of the principal is pivotal because he sets the stage and redirects attitudes toward a more contemporary approach to parent-teacher relationships. He constantly restructures situations with parents and teachers so that both groups view parent-teacher relationships in light of changing community needs.

When a school district begins to integrate populations through bussing, the principal should plan as far ahead for a smooth intermingling of student and parent populations as time permits. If he has been doing his job well, positive attitudes toward racial understandings have been developed. The principal should plan for meetings of representative P.T.A. members and other local leaders of both the white community and the black one that will be bussing its children. Organizational procedures should be jointly worked out and agreed upon using the widest possible parent base. Teachers through in-service workshops should have the greatest possible exposure to the latest data on integrated schools and they should be actively involved in planning for the transition. Their commitment is necessary for a successful program. Students should be involved in discussions, lessons and understandings so that they may better be ready for the new school year. Leadership on the part of the president of the P.T.A. should effect changes in the executive board to provide for the incoming parents. In these ways the P.T.A. becomes a potent force in the school community working with school leaders on real problems.

CHAPTER THIRTEEN

Viewed from the

Clothes Line

The author brought together three parents, who have appeared in earlier case conferences in this book, and engaged them in dialogue. The principal in dialoguing with these parents has drawn out some of the important things that parents look for in parent-teacher conferences.

The dialogue not only reveals insights these parents have about parent-teacher conferences, but also enables the reader to relate this information with that in the earlier conferences where these three parents reflected their concerns.

Principal: "I have asked that we sit down together to talk about the kinds of things that you as parents look for in a parent-teacher conference."

Mrs. J: "Well, for myself it is very important to have the teacher show that she has a real awareness of my child. This is best done by highlighting something specific that she has accomplished. For example, if my daughter knows more about rockets than anyone else in the class then I would like to be told. To go home after the conference and face the neighbors is a real problem no matter whether your child is doing very well, all right or poorly. If I had information on how well my child is doing in learning say about rockets, I then would have something tangible to say. Ideally, we parents would like the conferences to be very private affairs between the teacher and the parents, but we all know this is not the case."

Mrs. H: "The teacher should tell the parent what is being taught in science and social studies. She should show work samples for different months and evaluate the child's progress rather than the usual 'doing well' and 'no problems.'"

Mrs. M: "I would like to say how pleased I am with my child's teacher. He is definitely willing and able to work along with us. I have gained insights into my son's progress. I now understand fully the work he is doing. This has brought me closer to an awareness of his potential.

"I also like getting better acquainted with the teacher."

Mrs. J: "Yes, when the teacher tells you about your child's specific strengths and weaknesses and how she is helping to do something about them, then you as a parent know there is less chance of later parent-teacher misunderstandings."

Principal: "Are you ladies saying that you want concrete indications of your child's work?"

Mrs. J: "Yes, I find that by coming face to face with the teacher their is less chance of misinterpretation. When the teacher has on hand evidence of the child's work it backs up her comments."

Mrs. H: "I think that it is important to have personal contact with teachers. One gets a fuller picture of what goes on in the classroom. The parent then can get an impression of the teacher and her methods.

"I was able to discuss little problems that were bothering my child. Without the conference they would have gone unnoticed by the teacher."

Mrs. M: "I believe that my son's teacher can often tell me things about my child that I would never realize. He works with the children a large portion of the day and he certainly knows them. He has shown me where my child needs help and where we can help at home."

Mrs. J: "Yes, I would agree, if constructive advice is given. I would want to know how I could help my child achieve her full potential. Telling someone that her child can and should be doing better and not offering some solutions immediately gets my back up. Certainly, having a negative attitude at the onset of a conference accomplishes nothing!

"More information and time is needed at a conference, and more opportunities to discuss problems as they occur, not later."

Principal: "Are we saying that a helpful interchange of ideas between parent and teacher enables the parent to inform the teacher of home attitudes which in turn gives the teacher more insights into the attitude of the child in school?"

Mrs. M: "Yes, I would agree. I have gained a great deal from my conferences. I really wasn't giving my child the credit he deserved."

Mrs. J: "Well, I have found that after a conference I could measure the teacher's evaluation of my child against my own evaluation. After all, if a parent has a normal child, she would expect the child to do well in school or else there is something wrong with the school."

Principal: "It is true that once the parent and the teacher work together in mutual respect an overall understanding of the child's academic and emotional level can be arrived at.

"A healthy give and take between teacher and parent should develop a positive partnership.

"Would each of you in summing up this discussion state the most important thing that you look for in a conference?"

Mrs. J: "Yes, I look for a teacher who can show me that she truly understands my child and can point out areas where she is working to help my daughter."

Mrs. H: "I look for indications of improvement in the academic areas. Too often the teacher talks about social adjustment and behavior problems. My husband and I are interested in our boy's learning."

Mrs. M: "I seek out ways in which I may help my son improve in his school work. A teacher who can encourage him to work harder and reach his potential is my ideal."

The reader in referring to earlier case studies readily recognizes these three parents.

Mrs. J's concerns are about her daughter's adjustment to school. Mrs. J, like most parents, highlights the emphasis placed on a truly understanding teacher.

The consideration uppermost in a parent's mind is "does the teacher understand and have an empathy for my child?" If the child is happy in school, the parent is generally supportive of the teacher.

There are unfortunately some teachers who relate very well to children but who do not have many skills in teaching the subject areas. A number of these teachers perceive the teaching job as one of making the child emotionally comfortable in class and little more.

An administrator may find it difficult to motivate a teacher who considers himself a "good Joe" and who has community backing and yet doesn't put forth the effort to perfect his teaching skills.

The other side of the coin is also common where the teacher is a very fine craftsman but lacks the ability to relate well to the students. These teachers are often pressured by parents who feel that their children are not happy in class and are overworked.

The concern that Mrs. J has about the conference not being a private affair requires a considerable amount of parent orientation. If the parent uses confidential conference information and report card marks as a way of projecting her own status position, then the reason for these things is misunderstood. Likewise, if the parent must be defensive about her child's achievement when talking with other parents, there is certainly a lack of understanding of child growth and development.

The critical approach used by Mrs. J when she states that "telling someone that her child can and should be doing better and not offering some solutions immediately gets my back up" is not too uncommon in the suburban-metropolitan area.

The phone conversation which begins with, "I'm very disappointed about" and ends with the parent feeling better is an indication of an approach where the schoolman is initially placed on the defensive.

This pattern of taking a critical approach toward a school situation fits in with the anxious, rushed mode of life in suburbia and it should be seen more as a way that people have of approaching problems than as real feelings about the school.

Actually, most parents are reasonably pleased with the suburban school and when they protest, usually by voting down school budgets or by being antagonistic toward school personnel, they are voicing their frustrations about their own life problems.

Most parents feel powerless about affecting national events, but they can swing a school election or effect other changes on a local level.

Mrs. H places her foremost interest in the teacher's ability to improve the child's academic understandings.

Many parents stress test results, papers well done and the bringing home of A's on the report card.

The teacher would do well to present concrete evidence of marked improvement or the need for additional help where evident.

The teacher should stress the overall school orientation which would include the importance of the student's social and emotional growth.

As the parent understands the total educational effort, the emphasis will not be placed on A's but on the unique growth patterns of each child with the concomitant emotional, social, physical and academic evaluations.

This attitudinal change will take time and the orientation must be geared not only to the children and to the mother but to the father as well.

Mrs. H gives little acknowledgment to these vital areas partly because she does not know how to handle her son's behavior and also because her husband leaves the child rearing to his wife.

This important area of joint parent responsibility is highlighted in the cases of many suburban boys who rarely see their fathers. The mother is placed in the difficult position of assuming both the male and the female adult roles. Many normal young male behavior patterns which would not be highlighted in a family where both the father and mother participate, become major issues in a matrilineal suburban home.

The father is often overlooked on the elementary level because he is not readily available. This is most unfortunate as he does influence the attitudes of the children.

The father who works in a competitive world finds it very difficult to think in terms of the child's competing against himself rather than against others in the class. On the other hand, he sometimes equates the child's school world with a world of women, children and the safety of his suburban home rather than with the exploration of real life problems.

Schools would do well to have evening meetings where both

fathers and mothers may be present to develop further understandings of child growth concepts rather than leaving the orientation to
the mothers alone.

Mrs. M, like most parents, is seeking out specific ways that she
may help her son improve in school. She needs the reassurance that
Bill is working up to his capacity and that although he may not do
as well academically as his older brother, he will be able to find a
good place in society.

It might have been easier for Mrs. M to accept Bill if his brother
were less successful in school and the family were not in such an
upward-mobile position.

Little has been said about Bill's father and it would be well if
both the teacher and the principal work with both parents to develop an awareness of Bill's potential.

The classroom teacher had made progress with giving Mrs. M
a better understanding of Bill so that by the time she met with the
other parents and the principal, her attitude toward Bill's school
work had begun to change.

The school principal as the prime mover of this meeting was able
to elicit feelings from the parents that pinpoint their ideas about
parent-teacher conferences.

He is moving in the direction of recognizing the need for parents to discuss lay participation in areas where in the past only
professionals were involved.

He is still under the influence of an earlier pedantic orientation
when he states that, "It's true that once the parent and the teacher
work together in mutual respect an overall understanding of the
child's academic and emotional level can be arrived at." He con-
tinues this approach by saying that, "A healthy give and take between teacher and parent should develop a positive partnership."

He may be viewed as an administrator who is beginning to make
the transition from a paternalistic school leader to a contemporary,
educational change agent. He is aware that he holds a strategic and
a pivotal position with the parents.

I have collected and here present to the reader comments made
by parents after parent-teacher conferences in the belief that direct
statements may better express parent feelings:

"I learned nothing that I wasn't already aware of."

"The personal touch makes a difference in parent-teacher relationships."

"I enjoyed the individual attention."

"The teacher didn't seem to understand what my child was doing. She expected me to become a teacher at home."

"The meeting was direct and to the point. It was satisfactory for the first encounter."

"It really didn't inform me of too much of anything."

"The teacher was very candid in her evaluation."

"I like it when the teacher shows a willingness to discuss the parent's view of her child."

"You really get to know what your child is doing in class."

"I look for evidence that the teacher understands and likes my child."

"The teacher is a credit to her profession."

"It gave me a better insight into my child's ability and progress."

"I feel that my child is being given every opportunity to learn. If she does not do well, perhaps the home, not the school, should make some changes."

"I appreciate the teacher's interest, enthusiasm and understanding."

"When I speak to a teacher for a few minutes it is always more worthwhile than a thousand written words."

"I learned all I wanted to know."

These "live comments" reflect the wide range of statements that parents make after parent-teacher conferences.

The parent who states, "I learned nothing that I wasn't already aware of," tells the reader that she really didn't get anything out of the conference. The parent who states, "I like it when the teacher shows a willingness to discuss the parent's view of her child," shows a positive feeling toward the conference.

CHAPTER FOURTEEN

Keeping Up with Changes

in Education

The frustrations of an alert parent in a less than adequate school system are presented in this chapter. Unfortunately, there are some school systems which have not thought out some of the real problems in education, as this chapter makes evident.

The parent is correct when she states, "I don't think you are giving your parents enough credit. Because even though many of them never had formal education, they know how their children come home from school. They know if they're happy, they know if they're excited and they know what they like and what they don't like, and it might be very well for the school people to give an ear to these parents because they are educating these people's children."

An alert parent can of course work through the P.T.A., the school board and through interested civic groups to encourage new and exciting ideas for the school system. Yet if there are few interested people in the community, many of those real ideas fall on barren ground.

The school system mentioned here has rested on its laurels for many years and it has not been alert to the new people that are coming into the community with dynamic ideas.

This is all the more reason for the principal and his staff to be aware of changes in education and to keep in step with changing times.

127

Don't Make Waves!

Case no. 43H

Principal: "Good morning, Mrs. H. This is Miss R. I don't know if you have met our Supervisor."

Mrs. H: "Yes, I believe I met you the night of open school."

Miss R: "It's nice to see you again Mrs. H."

Principal: "I understand you have some concerns and you have asked to meet with us."

Mrs. H: "Yes, I really feel very hesitant in coming here because I have been in teaching and I don't like to go into a school and voice my opinion. I really do have some deep concerns and I think the first one is about your report card system. I know that you are not directly responsible because this is a dictate that comes from above, but I don't know quite how to explain my feelings about this. I just don't like to be the one to have to request a conference. Your reporting system to the parents leaves much to be desired. Your report gives a grade and sometimes there are comments and sometimes there aren't. A conference must be requested by the teacher and this tells me very little about my child. I take the responsibility of calling up and asking if there is a problem. I don't want to be the pushy parent, to have to come in and hear about my child. I don't know how you feel about this."

Principal: "We have talked as a staff about permitting parents to come in to see us and to voice all the concerns they have. However, we have not at this point felt it was necessary to have a specific time set aside for conferences. Now, we may get to that and I know some of the neighboring school systems have conference times in lieu of the report cards. What do you think, Miss R?"

Miss R: "Well, have you ever been refused a conference by a teacher if you have requested one?"

Mrs. H: "No, because my child is only a first grader. He is in Miss Z's class and I never had this school experience before. My son was in another school district last year and conferencing was a part of the total program, so I was very comfortable about it. Here I feel I would like to know about what level he is working at, his ability, his reaction to other children and his interaction with all those people he comes into contact with. I don't want to be the one to ask and seem like a "pushy mother."

Miss R: "Well, I hope that our teachers would not consider that and would certainly at your request be glad to see you and not consider you 'a pushy mother,' but rather one who is very interested. They might appreciate your coming in and your interest in your child."

Mrs. H: "I have to disagree with you Miss R. I don't like to be the one to have to instigate this. I think this should be part of the total school program for parent-school relationships, and I think you can learn an awful lot about the child. A teacher can help her own understanding of the child by having a conference with the parent. I would like to see some move towards this. I don't know what powers you have. I don't know what you can do, but it seems to me that you might do well to speak to some of your higher-ups about a program like this. Of course, I am just voicing my opinion. I know there is nothing you can do; this has got to be a school policy and I go on to my . . ."

Miss R: "I quite agree with you and under the circumstances and the system we are working with, you should feel free to contact the teacher, and I think our teachers would feel comfortable about talking with you. Whether you have a concern or not it will be just more information about your child and you can share what you know about your child with the teacher."

Mrs. H: "But don't you think other parents feel very much like myself and why shouldn't they have the same opportunity?"

Miss R: "I would agree with you and as you said your ideas are right. I think you should feel comfortable about going to the teacher or asking for an appointment and, perhaps, if more parents do that, we will see the need for structuring conferences regularly."

Mrs. H: "Well, let's see if I can arouse thirty other parents. Maybe our teachers will be very busy for the next couple of months."

Principal: "Mrs. H brings us a very fine suggestion, and because she is a professional teacher, she is pinpointing one of the concerns we have had in the district and maybe we are not moving as fast as we should. Maybe we should be thinking about the new innovations that are going on and I know some of the neighboring schools do have them. I would agree with Miss R; bear with us at this time and contact the teacher. Now, I would gather that of course you are concerned about the regular parent conference time. I would think there are other things that really bother you and this is just a slight thing."

Mrs. H: "Yes, I think you are very perceptive in what you say because along with that is my concern about the math situation in the school. I speak only for my own son because I know what's happening in his class, but of course living in a community where you have friends with children in school you find out what those youngsters are doing. I was interested to know that there is little or no grouping in the math program. Children are taught math rather homogeneously. The teacher will teach all the children the same page at the same time. I assume that any conscientious teacher will help an individual child along the way. She will provide for individual differences because this is part of teacher training, but it doesn't seem logical to me that children can all learn at the same rate and be taught effectively and efficiently in such a large group. The classes are quite large; I believe you have over thirty in your first grade, and it just doesn't make sense that you would group for reading and not for math when both are tool subjects and both require a certain amount of skill. You recognize it in one area and yet it doesn't seem to be recognized in another. I was questioning your philosophy on that."

Principal: "Of course, Mrs. H really raises a lot of real concerns that we have. I would also like Miss R to brief us a little bit on what we are doing in math. I think Eric is in the first grade."

Mrs. H: "First grade."

Principal: "So that here again, although certain individual differences are most important, there are other kinds of concerns that we have, such as identifying children's needs at this point. Would you like to say a few words about that, Miss R?"

Miss R: "Well, I think we have come quite a way in terms of understanding a reading concern and grouping for reading, and I would tend to agree with you that we should be doing much the same thing in math and spending equally as much time and effort on it. Unfortunately, we do not, and we find our teachers cannot manage five reading groups and five math groups at the same time; so they have perhaps sacrificed something in math instruction. I agree that all children begin at some point in math. As you said, where individual help was needed, they tried to keep the class together. Perhaps at some future time, we will be able to do much the same thing in math as we are doing in reading."

Mrs. H: "I would hope so because I hate to sound snippy, but the child came in knowing a little bit more than he is going out of the class knowing. He forgot all that his friends have taught him at home; he went through a first-grade program with a neighbor of mine where he lived last year. He has been playing with older children and he knew his numbers and he knew addition and he knew the sets long before he began first grade, and I don't push this at home. I don't believe it's my place to, but there are children who pick these things up and it's unfortunate he didn't progress at the same rate in school as he did out of school."

Principal: "You mentioned he learned much of this at a neighbors. Would you help us on that?"

Mrs. H: "Well, he has friends who are very bright students and they love to play school; it was last winter that they spent a good deal of time at my house and the boy's house. There were three of them. Two had gone to first grade . . . excellent students, and mine was in kindergarten. They would bring their homework and their books home and I taught him everything that he is presently learning. In fact, fortunately they weren't using the same material because that would have been disastrous. He is not bored. I cannot say he is bored. He is very happy. He is a very well-adjusted child but I was hoping he would progress a little further. He spent weeks learning cardinal and ordinal numbers and he was doing that in kindergarten. He had a kindergarten teacher who taught them mathematical concepts when he was in his other school district."

Principal: "If I may add a thought. He also learned reading at home before he came to school?"

Mrs. H: "No, he could not read when he came to first grade."

Principal: "I see, but as far as math goes . . ."

Mrs. H: "Math, yes."

Principal: "As far as math goes, he did get prior instructions and when he came to school, he was aware of some of the concepts."

Mrs. H: "His math concepts far exceed his reading concepts. He didn't . . . he was not reading when he started school; nothing more than any other child in kindergarten had."

Principal: "Now when you spoke to the classroom teacher about this, did you get any indication of the kinds of things she could do to help the child?"

Mrs. H: "She just said she has a very large class and that Eric does beautifully in math. That's all she said."

Principal: "I see."

Miss R: "I think Eric is unusual in what he came to school with."

Mrs. H: "Yes, right."

Miss R: "Very few first graders have concepts and backgrounds similar to his."

Mrs. H: "Usually they come with reading skills but this was one of those . . . he likes numbers. He could spend hours counting and counting money. He loves to collect money. He likes it. I think he would rather do that than read."

Principal: "I wonder if there are any kinds of projects, Miss R, that a teacher may get involved with in terms of amount."

Miss R: "There are some things for Eric on an individual basis. Certainly, there are some program materials that he might be able to handle if we had them available. There are some program materials, if he were able to read and some of them without reading material, but the teacher would have to be able to present him with it and perhaps he could work as an individual."

Mrs. H: "I really don't want that! I think he should be part of a group and there must be other youngsters on his level who can do what he can do and who are as interested in this area as he is. I don't want to make him an exception. This is why I don't push or why I don't ask for conferences and this is why I feel as I do about the total picture—grouping, conferencing for everyone, not just for my child."

Principal: "You are raising some very interesting points, especially as a professional teacher. At this point our school system has not, at least on a primary level, thought about grouping for math. Although there may be other children in the room who are ready for this kind of experience, we have not as yet been able to identify them. If maybe, Miss R—she works with the teacher—could look into this further and see what kind of help we could give Eric. I know what you are saying and I know some neighboring schools do grouping, but we just haven't reached that point yet and I am a little embarrassed to say so. Now, when you spoke with the teacher, I gather, she did mention to you that we have very large class sizes."

Mrs. H: "Yes, I could see that from my visit that evening. You are overcrowded, understaffed and you have a shortage of materials. I have never seen such a scant library, especially after coming from several other school districts that had so much more. The materials are few and far between as compared with other places that I have visited. I know that there are budgetary problems. I just think that maybe . . . . My suggestions don't require money, just a little thought and change."

Principal: "Well, I think you have a good point here. Once again, with the large number of children, we have not as yet reached a point where we can start to think of individualizing our program. What other concerns did you have?"

Mrs. H: "Well, my third and I would think, perhaps, the least important concern is reading because if a child can read I think he can be enhanced at home and he can get along on his own. But one thing still bothers me a little bit and that is this lockstep method of reading—the child is exposed to a basal reading program and once he completes it, he cannot have supplementary reading at that level or at the next level. He then must stay within the grade structure until the following year when he is allowed to go to second grade in a basal program even though his reading skills far exceed the skills being given at the second grade. It's redundant, it's repetitious, and I feel it holds back a child, but I said I am not as concerned about this as I am about the other things because he will get it anyway. It just might bore some children. I am not saying it has bored mine. He is not; but perhaps, primary grade children are not bored easily anyway. But it might hamper children later on and I don't think it opens up the vistas that you can open up if you just take the lid off the reading program. Let children proceed at their own rate—have their supplementary reading and still continue getting the basal structure without being locked into a grade level. That's my objection."

Principal: "Of course, one of the immediate concerns I have as an administrator thinking about this is that we would run into problems with the junior high school. In other words, if we committed our teachers to teach children, as you say, on their level—and I think you've got a very interesting philosophic point here—I can see where the seventh grade teacher could become very, very concerned as the children graduate into junior high and find that some of the material has already been covered. This may be a big problem and I think this is why a lot of our teachers like the basal reader because they believe that the work is outlined for them: this is the grade work; this is where the child belongs, and if we move them ahead we may make the teacher on the next grade level very uncomfortable and place her in an unusual position. Do you have any comment, Miss R?"

Miss R: "Well, I think you said it all very well, but I might add too that perhaps some of the skills material in the basal program can be handled by the child with reading matter. Some of it on a concept level and some of it on an understanding level, is sometimes beyond what the child can handle or maybe not beyond what he can handle but not necessarily within his realm of real understanding."

Mrs. H: "Well, I don't think that this will be found true if tried. I believe there are tests that go along with your basal reading. If a child doesn't have the conceptual ability and this is true if his maturity is not up to it, then I feel it would show up and at that point you could say to a parent, 'Well, I am sorry Mrs. so-and-so, your child reads but he doesn't read with understanding. He cannot relate, he cannot transfer his learning and he is not ready to be moved to the next level.' But until you try this and see what this child is capable of doing, I think you're doing the child a terrible injustice."

Miss R: "I think it takes a tremendous area of testing, having materials available and the time to do all these things for all these children. As I said, many children can read the words and even have a fairly good amount of comprehension and yet innuendoes, the concepts, the way the sentences are structured, they never really quite get the full meaning from it if the material is just a little bit above them. Their own maturity, their achievement, and their ability are important factors. They don't have the maturity to handle this kind of thing."

Mrs. H: "Then you are saying, testing would show it."

Miss R: "Some testing does and some doesn't, and finding this out would require a great deal of time and effort and materials."

Mrs. H: "Miss R, I am paying $1,800.00 a year in taxes and I would assume that my money would be paying for quality education and if this is what is required for quality education, then maybe some of the money that is being spent for other things, such as sports and extraneous other help, should be siphoned into the educational program."

Miss R: "Well, of course, I cannot but agree with you."

Mrs. H: "Yes, I realize but I am a little angry about this."

Miss R: "But maybe becoming active in our community, seeing our school board and getting to know the people who make the decisions about these kinds of things will help. Certainly, our interest is the same as yours; the children in the school and quality education for them."

Mrs. H: "Right. What you are trying to say to me is that you really agree but your hands are tied and you don't have the money to give the kind of individualized instruction and program that perhaps would be better and that you really don't disagree with me philosophically. Is that what you are trying to tell me?"

Miss R: "You might say that, yes."

Principal: "I wonder when you talked to the teacher about Eric's reading what she told you and what other kinds of reading material she may be using with Eric other than the basic reader?"

Mrs. H: "Yes, I asked her and she gave me a list of supplementary books because I said I do bring books home occasionally from school and I don't want to bring home anything that he would be exposed to. I have the list with the exception of three out of ten or twelve for first grade supplementary books. Three of them were easy second grade, and I did see them. They are nice books. I think he should read them and be exposed to them, but he could read those half asleep and so could the other children in his group. Why can't they be exposed more? You know as well as I do that reading is exposure and it's repetition and it's constant practice and enjoyment. Why can't they be exposed to new vocabulary? Their phonetics is good; they could sound out new words. My objection is their being locked into a grade situation. I don't think that it's fair to any child, nor is it fair to the children at the other end of the scale because they are being shortchanged."

Principal: "Well, I would say first of all that one of the big problems that we have in a K–12 district is the concern that the junior high would have when our children following your plan get to the junior high level. Here again the teacher up there may have to go through a lot of repetition. I can see where Miss R could sit down with the teacher and discover what other kinds of materials may be used with Eric. You have mentioned that his reading is not as advanced as his math, but I could see getting into books other than the basal texts."

Mrs. H: "Oh, I do too."

Principal: "But if we use, for instance, a second grade basal, then the second grade teacher would be hard pressed when she goes to teach the book, and you can imagine as a teacher how you would feel if the teacher on the grade below you actually had covered some of your work."

Mrs. H: "Why must the teacher on the second grade level teach second grade? Why can't she teach the third grade?"

Principal: "Well, I would say if she wanted to teach the third grade, then she should transfer to the third grade because we have the grade so well worked out, so finely developed, that each grade is a body of knowledge to fit the chronological age of the child."

Mrs. H: "You really distress me because if you are putting school organization ahead of children's progress and children's welfare, then this is a sad commentary on education today and I am very disappointed. I cannot begin to tell you how unhappy I am. After all, if the colleges were to take that approach, then we would not have any reason for honors courses in the high school. But many of the students do go into college and pre-college courses and the high schools do give the children a lot more than they offered twenty years ago. It would be a sad day in this country if we were to hold back everyone for the sake of organization."

Principal: "Of course, I am not talking about the second grade as it was constituted twenty years ago. I am talking about a very advanced second grade which learns about rockets and about the fundamentals of geometry."

Mrs. H: "Yes, it goes back to reading about Tom and Jerry."

Principal: "Yes, we have had that series in our district for quite a while, although you know we have brought in some integrated material so that we haven't stayed completely with the old Tom and Jerry series. We have tried to be contemporary. I can say that. Miss

R, is there any way that in working with the teacher you possibly could set up a time when the three of you could talk about math? I think Mrs. H also might like to work through the P.T.A. and we may be able to talk about some additional materials that can be brought into the school."

Mrs. H: "Oh, our P.T.A. group in this district doesn't get involved with curriculum or anything to do with school activities. I don't know if you are aware of that. This is very much against the philosophy of the P.T.A."

Principal: "Yes. Well I am glad you mentioned that. Of course, here in our district we have felt it is better if parents do not get too involved in something that they are not familiar with; that is, curriculum. We have left that to the professionals and, of course, as we talk here we realize that you are wearing two hats; both the hat of a parent and of a professional teacher. So both Miss R and I take this into our thinking as we work with you. But you must agree that many of our parents are very, very skilled in housework and shopping and the like. I don't mean to be condescending, but when it comes to curriculum matters they are not equipped. Can you imagine what kind of situation we would have if we opened our doors to the public and allowed them to sit in on our curriculum committees? Why, the first thing they would want is to evaluate the teachers."

Mrs. H: "I don't think you are giving your parents enough credit. Because even though many of them never had formal education, they know how their children come home from school. They know if they're happy; they know if they're excited and they know what they like and what they don't like; it might be very well for the school people to give an ear to these parents because they are educating these people's children. I don't think you have to be a professional to know how your children are feeling about school and about what they are doing."

Principal: "Do you have any other comment, Miss R?"

Miss R: "I would strongly suggest, Mrs. H, that we set up a time where you, Mrs. Z and I can sit down and talk about Eric and your specific concern. I think our first area of concern would be both in math and in reading."

Mrs. H: "Very good."

Principal: "I would appreciate that and feel free always to come in because we may not have the most updated school system in the world, but we are people who do work hard at it."

Mrs. H: "I know you do. I do appreciate your position and I realize it's not you. It may very well be from above and I am aware of those problems."

Principal: "Well, thank you very much."

1. Do you think that parents should play a greater part in school matters?
2. Should curriculum development be strictly the province of the professional?
3. How do you react to the principal's approach in this case?
4. If you were the teacher what would you do to help Mrs. H?
5. How do you feel about Mrs. H as a parent?
6. Should parents teach their children to read before they begin school?

Mrs. H, a well-informed parent and a professional teacher, presents many concerns to the principal and the supervisor.

She is definite, direct and quite specific. She wants individualized instruction for her child and in a larger scope she is pressing for instructional reform.

Mrs. H is a newcomer in a rather staid community which has experienced growth but has not attempted to change as some neighboring schools have. Mrs. H, although representing a progressive approach, is strictly in a minority and this lends to her frustration.

The principal sees curriculum in strictly graded terms and he shows a real concern when the parent talks about allowing the child to progress at his own rate. He is diametrically opposed to the parent who sees instruction on a continuum rather than as a body of knowledge limited to a chronological basis.

The supervisor is aware of the limitations of the school organization and, although she leans toward the parent in her thinking, she finds herself in a most difficult position. She can best help by working directly with the parent and the teacher within this limited framework.

Little can be done here until a ground swell of parent pressure is felt by the school administrators. Then and only then will real change come to this school district.

CHAPTER FIFTEEN

What Really

Bothers Father?

The concerned-father syndrome is not too common today because the mother generally assumes the role of the parent-school negotiator. When the father does become involved he generally wants some definite, clear answers as in the case of the father in this chapter.

It is well for the principal carefully to research the father's concern beforehand and to have all the available information on hand for the conference.

Some principals, after discussing the father's concern, will ask him to sit in on a lesson or on several lessons and to observe the class. Generally, fathers have a very vague idea of what is actually going on in today's classroom and a visit to the room may act as an eye-opener. It is well to arrange a visitation so that immediately after the visit the teacher, the principal and the father may sit down and discuss what happened in the classroom.

It is also important to give the father information that he can readily relay to his wife. In this way he can explain to her what the teacher is actually doing and how his child responded in class.

There are, of course, cases where the teacher may resent a parent coming into the room, and in this case the principal may want to limit the conference to discussing the problem with the parent in his office.

As teachers become more aware of parents' concerns, they are less hesitant to have visitors in the room.

Case no. 691L

Principal: "Good afternoon Mr. L. It's very nice to see you."

Mr. L: "Good afternoon. I know you are busy. I am, too, but we have to get certain things straight. I'm concerned about my son, Mark."

Principal: "Oh?"

Mr. L: "Yes, he is working with one child or even by himself in arithmetic and I don't see how this is a way of learning."

Principal: "I see. Could you tell me a little more about this?"

Mr. L: "Well, the teacher put him into a group and for weeks now he is just working by himself. I think he has a race with another boy. The teacher gives him pages to do and that's about it. He is forgotten except when the teacher says to do some more pages."

Principal: "I see. Did you have a chance to talk to the teacher about this?"

Mr. L: "Oh yes! I mentioned this and she said he is a bright boy and he is in his own group."

Principal: "I see."

Mr. L: "I just wonder how you feel about children, not only for a few days, but week after week working by themselves?"

Miss R: "Is this only in math, Mr. L?"

Mr. L: "Yes."

Miss R: "Does Mark have other kinds of experiences during the day with other children or with the teacher?"

Mr. L: "Yes. He is with three or four other children in reading."

Miss R: "Did the teacher give you any information of the kinds of things your son is doing? Have you gotten any remarks from Mark?"

Mr. L: "He is doing long division and multiplication. He is learning arithmetic, but that's not my concern because I know he will learn arithmetic. I want him to get the social interaction of learning and responding with other children which he is not getting by reading a page and attempting to figure it out by himself and now and then having a teacher come to see what it's all about. What I would like to know is what provisions we will be able to make in order to have him work with a group of children, not two or three, but some viable kind of a group."

Miss R: "Well, isn't he working with a group of children in social studies, in science, and in other areas as well?"

Mr. L: "I think if we could stick to math, we could work this out because math is a kind of thing you don't just memorize, but you ought to have an interaction."

Miss R: "There is some research on children learning certain skill subjects by the process Mark is using: self-explanation, self-discovery and learning by oneself without the need for interaction. Now it may be true that Mark needs interaction with other children, but there are certain areas of the curriculum which are skill subjects and which many children can learn in this way and learn well. I would agree, there should be social interaction."

Mr. L: "Math ought to be a live kind of subject, not just turning the page and reading a problem, doing it, turning to the back of a book and seeing if the answer is correct. It can involve everyday living and there's no provision being made for that in this school. This is why I am here. I am asking what type of provisions do you think you will be able to make so that this child who is most superior in math can go into a group and work on the level of arithmetic that he is at."

Principal: "I wonder if the teacher is working with Mark on a contract system, where she has identified some of his skills and where she is trying to help him on this level. I wonder, Miss R, if Mr. L feels concerned about social interaction which we would agree is very important. We can look into this and possibly we could include Mark in another group. I would like to know if the teacher has identified his skills and is working with him as an individual on a one-to-one basis. I would also like to know what other small groups there are because if you have a concern about social interaction, I think we could make some adjustment. Can you give us some information, Miss R?"

Miss R: "In an attempt to truly individualize instruction, more and more you will find children working on their own in particular skill areas. Perhaps, as you say it does something to change the nature of mathematics as we now view it. If this is our goal in teaching skills to children in a sequential order according to their ability, then I don't personally think that an individual learning by himself can be damaged provided there is social interaction."

Mr. L: "If we are thinking about teaching a sequential level of skills this way, I can't possibly believe that Mark is the only one in the school who is learning these particular skills. I would think that somewhere in the school, perhaps in some other group, there are children who are also learning this with a teacher. They would be able to interact with each other and then have all the benefits of the situation that I think we are looking for."

Principal: "In other words, Miss R is saying that the teacher has identified some of the skills of the student and has placed him in a one-to-one relationship in our individualized math program, and you're saying, Mr. L, that you feel the social relationship is so important that we should be able to work within such a framework and see it as part of the total configuration rather than simply in terms of math concepts."

Mr. L: "I would hope so! Miss R's idea of individualizing instruction in such a manner that it's almost one to one while putting stress on a subject area more than the type of thing that I hoped we would have in an elementary school seems silly."

Miss R: "Well, I would think that would be partially it. I also believe that we will reach a level of sophistication where we can determine which children can learn certain things on a purely individual basis and which cannot learn that way but must have interaction. Perhaps we aren't sophisticated enough really to determine that completely, but certainly I think time will show that there are children who do much better on an individual basis, and maybe the safest place to start it is in a skill area. I would have great concern if we were to become content-oriented and only worry about teaching math and not teaching other things that go along with it. I do think that under the limitations we work with in the public schools—the great number of children, their different styles, abilities and needs—we might be able to diagnose not only their skill needs but also their learning styles and determine which children can learn certain things better by themselves and which need a group situation in which to learn. We can't always make enough groups to suit everybody's needs."

Mr. L: "This is exactly why I feel that it might be easier on the teacher not to have an extra group with Mark. I think this other friend would work in well. Can you attempt to find the teacher who is working with her children on those levels and skills which Mark is presently working on, rather than his going page after page? Just simply intergrade him into that group, and I think you will find that he will progress well. He will also benefit more.

"This has not been two days or three days of an intensive kind of a thing. It has gone on now for three weeks or longer where the child has a page to do and then another."

Miss R: "May I ask what his reaction is to this?"

Mr. L: "When I ask him what the teacher says, if this answer is right or wrong, he usually replies, "Oh, she didn't get to me.""

Principal: "How old is Mark?"

Mr. L: "He will be nine in August."

Principal: "Well, I would suggest that Miss R check into this and we'll see what we can do about placing him in a group with several other children. What other concerns do you have?"

Mr. L: "Well perhaps this also is tied up with it. I know that the children go from teacher to teacher—I received a comment on the report card about Mark's reading skills and abilities that doesn't help me feel as if I know what's going on in the school. Of course, I can't always be here. Another one of your teachers made me feel a bit awkward because she said in arithmetic, Mark is doing nicely. If you received this coment in a school that is supposed to be ungraded, where they are working with children on all levels, and heard that your child is doing nicely, Miss R, what would you think your child is learning? What would you get out of it?"

Miss R: "Very little. I would want to know more."

Mr. L: "Yes, and when I asked the teacher for a chance to speak with her, she said, 'I don't know—he is doing nicely; what more can I tell?' Would you help me?"

Miss R: "Well, I would have to talk to Mark's teacher and find out what level he is working at and what his expectancy is and where he is in that respect. I couldn't answer without knowing Mark and knowing the situation."

Mr. L: "I'd like to know the subjects that he is learning, and where he is weak and strong. I'd like to know these types of things, rather than, 'he is a nice boy and we would like to have more like him.' "

Miss R: "You were not able to get the information you asked for?"

Mr. L: "You see, I wrote two notes. That was two weeks ago. People are busy and I didn't want to go over anyone's head. Nevertheless, having written two notes, I would like the courtesy of a reply."

Miss R: "Did you ask for a conference?"

Mr. L: "Oh yes! So far I think that we have two concerns. One, you are going to get him into a group which will work on his level where he can respond to a teacher rather than a page turning kind of a thing. I am sure now that you could set a time when we could know when it will be done; then this other thing about getting his report card straight."

Principal: "It may be a good idea if Miss R sets up a conference with the teacher. I will attend so that we can make certain the boy is in a correct social group. I think if I read your concern correctly, you consider the subject matter area important, but you see it within a context of social interaction."

Mr. L: "I don't mean to make it a ballroom kind of thing. What I am saying is that the two boys have work to do and it's almost next page, next page, next page and it's a race. I don't think it's that healthy. I would like to see him at times listen to other people's answers rather than have to draw out each one himself."

Principal: "Let me ask you a question, Mr. L. When your boy plays with others at home or is involved with the cub scouts or whatever, do you find that he gets a good amount of social inter-action?"

Mr. L: "Oh sure."

Principal: "But you feel that this is a very strong area as you work with your son so that you would want him to get as many social situations under his belt, so to speak, as he can."

Mr. L: "I think the stress is too much on social living in the classroom."

Principal: "But we are talking about interaction of people."

Mr. L: "Interaction of ideas, not just the social kind. An inter-action of the meaning of arithmetic—how one arrives at a particular answer."

Principal: "I see. I understand what you are saying now. Yes, if I may re-interpret because I think I misunderstood the question at first. You're not so concerned about the child being in a social sit-uation for the values that come out of this, although I think we would both agree this is important, but you are talking about the learner in terms of intellectual stimulation."

Mr. L: "Yes."

Principal: "This occurs when a number of people are together as opposed to an individual learning situation which may be very fine. But your thinking is, can we give him more of this interaction-stimulation kind of thing?"

Mr. L: "I would think this can be done almost the same way that we are conferring here. My idea is one idea. You have an idea. Now with an interaction, we can have more than one."

Principal: "Fine. I think we can arrange that without any difficulty. Now to go back to the second problem, and I think it's a rather important one. In the past when you've spoken to the teacher, have you found that you received rather generalized kinds of answers or have you been given specific data on your child?"

Mr. L: "I don't think the teacher really knows what she is doing. In fact it would be pretty embarrassing for her if I were to attend the conference that you intend to have with her because I was never able to get an idea of exactly where my son's skills are and I think she can't contend with that fact. She rather has to teach one whole class and just say 'here you two kids, you go do something.' "

Principal: "Let me ask you a question. Last year, did you find that Mark was in a situation where he received the kind of education that he needed?"

Mr. L: "Yes."

Principal: "But it's this year that you feel a concern."

Mr. L: "Yes."

Principal: "Alright. The next question is—have you had an opportunity to talk with the teacher about your concern? The reason why I mention it is that it's May and we only have five weeks of the school year left. Have you had an opportunity to confer with her and to talk with her?"

Mr. L: "Yes, I have but I haven't been—perhaps—negative towards my son. I was attempting to hold back because being in education myself I have this tendency not to push someone."

Principal: "I see."

Mr. L: "I think I don't push enough and I would rather have him go into a situation either for the remainder of the term where he can remember some better things than go into the situation next

WHAT REALLY BOTHERS FATHER?

term with a feeling—'Oh, here I go again.' Then you will be a better able to judge where he ought to be placed."

Principal: "I see. Do you have anything you want to add to that, Miss R?"

Miss R: "No, but I would very much like us to meet with the teacher."

Mr. L: "Would you like me to be there?"

Miss R: "Oh yes!"

Principal: "Definitely!"

Mr. L: "Well, then you can set up some time."

Miss R: "I'll speak to her, and we will call you to set up a time that's mutually convenient."

Mr. L: "I would hate to have her feel too badly about it, but I just don't think that she really knows what grouping is all about."

Principal: "I would appreciate your consideration of the May date and appeal to your sensitivity as a fellow teacher in not pressing the teacher unduly. But as you worked with the teacher over the course of the year and I gather that you and your wife possibly have been at conferences, did you leave the conference feeling rather empty?"

Mr. L: "With this particular teacher, yes."

Principal: "I see, and did you bring this up to her or talk about it so that she was aware of your concern?"

Mr. L: "I am sorry you ask that because I believe that any astute person aware of people's feelings would have caught them, but she didn't."

Principal: "I see. Well I think it's most important for us to meet. Here again I haven't been told about this and I don't know if Miss R knows anything about this situation. Whenever there is a concern with the teacher, of course, we would want to come in on the conference. Is this the homeroom teacher as well as the person who teaches math? Is she also the lady who teaches reading or . . ."

Mr. L: "No. Mark has someone else for reading and he has a homeroom teacher."

Principal: "But this is the lady who teaches math only?"

Mr. L: "That's right."

Principal: "I see. Alright, let me ask you another question. When you went into a conference with the homeroom teacher, did you feel it to be a worthwhile experience?"

Mr. L: "Not as bad as the math teacher."

Principal: "As the math teacher?"

Mr. L: "She can be very sweet."

Principal: "I see. What about the reading teacher? Have you been able to talk with her?"

Mr. L: "Yes. Not only was I able to talk with her, but I feel we have gotten some satisfaction, for upon my suggestion, she was only too happy to bootleg certain assignments. When I say bootleg, I mean to give him some extra ones, to toss in social studies with the reading rather than other things and he has been very happy with it. I do think that she is terrific. I've seen her work."

Principal: "Alright. The reason I asked is that I wanted to narrow it down; if there is a concern with the math teacher, Miss R and I can pinpoint this. We will work with her so our conference will be a four-way one where both of us will be in on it and we may be able to reach a better understanding and see just where we are."

Mr. L: "If I may defend her in this manner, I don't object to Mark having her as a teacher. If at some other time of the day, he can have her teaching a group that is learning the kinds of things he's learning, but that would be up to you."

Principal: "I don't quite follow you. I'm sorry."

Mr. L: "Well, she sees a variety of classes a day. The time Mark sees her, only Mark and six other boys are working at this kind of work. Maybe some other time of the day when she will be teaching from these pages, these skills, but to a larger group and then perhaps you could find out that he could somehow be shifted there or in with another teacher. I just think that her perception of what group work is, needs to be sharpened."

Miss R: "I would like to look into this further, and we will speak with her and see what levels and groups she has and how many children she's working with at that time."

Mr. L: "Yes. I think it's all part of the second half of this problem."

Miss R: "There are also times we work within teams, and for the sake of being able to share information and evaluate children, we prefer keeping students within the team. Although I am not completely familiar with it, I admit I should be. The possibilty is that within this team, there is no other group. I don't know. Perhaps this is the solution or a way of instructing or having Mark be close to mathematical concepts on his level rather than sitting through a group lesson that is not. Now certainly if it's not answering the needs of the child socially or psychologically then it's just not worth worrying about his math skills at that point if other things are not going right."

Mr. L: "Oh, maybe we can worry about both and somehow, I am sure, you could effect a change whereby one of these two children could be put in a group with other children who are learning."

Miss R: "That may not always be possible."

Mr. L: "Well, it may be food for thought."

Miss R: "Yes."

Principal: "Is this little boy a friend of Mark?"

Mr. L: "They know each other from school. They don't play too much together. They live about a mile apart. I just see it as too much competition. There is too much racing to see who can get ahead, because these aren't thoughts anymore but pages. And being capable and being good children, they're relatively still—they'll be quiet; they won't cause much trouble. But I don't think they see the teacher or the teacher sees them enough to really get . . . to have an understanding of what is going on in their minds—the processes of learning. Only answers come out."

Miss R: "I would be very concerned Mr. L if this were the case and if the children were doing page after page. I would tend to agree with you and I would certainly want to look into it because if we are using this technique as a means to individualize, we should be very certain of what we are doing—what kinds of children we are working with and what best suits their needs, not only in ability but in style."

Mr. L: "I realize we can't individualize to the utmost degree. I wouldn't. I don't even think you would be doing well having the teacher jump around or look for a different skill here and there. I would like to reiterate, what I would like is to see my son with a group of children who will be able to explore the intricacies and the involvement in some math skills, so they can share ideas and arrive at the same solution but in different ways."

Principal: "Would you be opposed to any kind of learning experience where your child may be working alone over any period of time, about one to two weeks, in any specific kind of situation?"

Mr. L: "No, not if he understood there was a certain goal, but there's no goal here because it would go on and on forever in arithmetic."

Principal: "Of course, if you are in agreement or you say this would be alright, then wouldn't this also negate your statement that the interaction, the cerebral interaction of people working together, exchanging ideas is a kind of ideal that you are looking for?"

Mr. L: "Were you speaking of skills?"

Principal: "Yes. It could be skills; it could be other things. As I understood you, you talked about the importance of people interacting in the learning situation. My question to you is: Would you feel uncomfortable if your child was on a one-to-one basis with the teacher rather than in interaction with a number of children working together on a problem?"

Mr. L: "I don't even think a private school could give a one-to-one interaction over such a long period of time with the teacher. One of the reasons I've come here is that the teacher herself does not get to see my son."

Principal: "I see. So it's more than just the concern for an interaction of people learning the problem together. In other words, what you are questioning is the procedure that the teacher is using. Is this a rote kind of thing or is it really meaningful?"

Mr. L: "That's it."

Principal: "But you're not opposed to a child working alone with the teacher over a period of time?"

Mr. L: "Children work alone with their hobbies sometimes."

Principal: "Fine. You are not questioning that. What you are questioning is the teacher presenting this in a rote fashion."

Mr. L: "Yes. I am attempting to bring to your attention a situation which is really not yet out of hand in your school, but I would hate to see it happen. You have either a problem on one extreme or the other and you just put it aside."

Principal: "Well alright. I think we understand this a little better, and I think what Miss R will do is to look into this. I would suggest that she do some observation in the classroom. I would also suggest she sit down with the teacher to further find out the kinds of things and the way she is presenting them to your boy and then we'll have a four-way meeting, and I can assure you, we will give it our very close attention.

"Thank you for coming."

1. Do you have any reaction to the approach Mr. L uses in presenting his problem?
2. Do you believe Mr. L has a justifiable concern?
3. Should parents be given an understanding of the problems and concerns in initiating instructional programs?
4. If you were Mark's teacher, how would you approach Mr. L?

Mr. L, a concerned parent, is made to feel comfortable enough to speak freely about his instructional concerns. He tends to be negative about the school and the teacher, and he asumes that he knows what the schools should do. He is free with suggestions.

It appears that Mr. L is being argumentative for its own sake rather than to achieve understanding of his concerns. It would seem that Mr. L is seeking out an arena to sound out his ideas.

Does this become a game of words and an outlet for a "teacher-turned-parent"?

I question the information presented by the supervisor, Miss R, in that she becomes very involved in the program to the point where I suspect Mr. L will use some of this data later as ammunition to use against the school and the teacher.

The question of how much to involve the parent in the internal problems of the school comes into sharp focus as the supervisor questions how to balance social groups with instructional problems.

It would have been better if the supervisor viewed Mr. L more as a parent and less as a fellow teacher.

Sometimes many other problems and fears that parents have are opened up with this kind of philosophical discussion whereas the direct concerns presented by the parent may better be handled by dealing with the question simply and directly.

CHAPTER SIXTEEN

The Superintendent Wore

High-buttoned Shoes

This chapter deals with a school system whose superintendent is not keeping up with educational change. As the reader follows the dialogue, he will become more aware that the superintendent is the key man who either encourages innovation and change or else stifles it.

Unfortunately, some superintendents build a small army of supporters about them and view change as a threat to their position. The school principal in this dialogue constantly defends his superintendent, yet the reader suspects that the principal is uncomfortably cast in this role.

It is the responsibility of the school board and an enlightened citizenry to have the kind of leadership at the helm that works toward positive change through a staff of teachers and principals that is permitted to explore and to research the latest innovations in education.

The superintendent needs to surround himself with staff members who can constructively criticize his administration rather than act as "yes" men. This requires a school board tolerant of honest mistakes and ready to accept the top man as a real leader.

Case no. 156N
Principal: "Well, good afternoon, Dr. N. How are you?"
Dr. N: "It's very nice of you to take the time to see me."

Principal: "I haven't seen you in a while. I know you have a little boy in our school. Is there anything I can help you with?"

Dr. N: "Well, I didn't really want to see you about this because you're a fellow principal. I know you are busy, but I have a boy who is presently in your fourth grade and he has a little bit of a problem in math. He has very fine math ability, yet all through school his teachers have seen fit to have him work the basic math text with the rest of the class. It seems to be a whole class approach to learning. No class all through his school career in your building has gone beyond the textbook pages. Even though he does appear to have great ability in math he has not been challenged."

Principal: "You say he hasn't gone beyond the textbook page. Are you referring to any particular book that he is working on? I mention that because as you know in our present curriculum, which is carefully defined by our central office, we have a whole series of textbooks that are well developed by some of the finest mathematicians and writers in the country. I was wondering if you had a concern about the pages he was working on or what? I want to help you."

Dr. N: "Quite frankly, I think he is bored stiff."

Principal: "Oh!"

Dr. N: "He gets exactly the same assignment in the basic math book that all the rest of the students do—right from the below-average students up to students close to his caliber. So it's a little bit of a concern to me. He has great ability. We were working in my other school system on a math adoption program and I brought home some sample books at one time. He was able before he entered kindergarten to go through the second grade math book. He worked every problem in the book."

Principal: "May I ask you a question about that? When you say he worked every problem to second grade, did he have difficulty in reading the book?"

Dr. N: "Well, I'm sorry. I'm only referring to the drill examples such as adding and subtracting."

Principal: "Oh, I see. In other words, when he entered kindergarten, he had a good understanding of some of the basic math concepts."

Dr. N: "Oh, yes."

Principal: "And the basic functions?"

Dr. N: "Yes. He always counted the juice money for the teacher."

Principal: "I see. Now as far as his math ability goes, did you have an opportunity to help him in mathematics before he came to school?"

Dr. N: "Well, I'll tell you how this worked. We always insisted after school that he take a nap every afternoon, so we put him to bed. However, he would almost never sleep. It seemed to be his style. So for Christmas one year, we gave him what is referred to as an add and count scale—an educational toy with plastic numbers. You've probably seen them."

Principal: "Yes."

Dr. N: "He would work and balance the numbers. The numbers were weighted in size and weight as to their value. For example, you put a six and a three on one side of the scale and balance it with a nine on the other side. It seemed that he picked up a lot of basic combinations and concepts from this type of thing. This was pretty much on his own without any help from me. However, I did bring him home a 100 chart where you have ten rows of ten on one side up to 100 and up to 200 on the opposite side of the sheet. I showed him how you can count on the number lines by adding groups, putting them together and how to get the total the same way with subtracting. One other thing I did with him was to explain tens by grouping toothpicks and showing him that concept, but beyond that point, aside from going into his room when he went to bed at night and giving him numbers to add in his head, I did no work with him formally."

Principal: "I see. Now you are an unusual parent. Most of our parents at least in this area, don't give their children that kind of a background and I would say that if we had a number of parents who motivated their children before kindergarten, we would probably want to do special things with the small group. You can understand I am sure the problem we would have if we tried to give special help to each individual child who had a special problem or a special interest. I could see the first grade teacher being quite busy with this kind of procedure especially with thirty children, but if you could suggest something, I would be glad to . . ."

Dr. N: "I am not asking for complete individual attention, but I do happen to know that any good teacher who has grouped in reading would certainly realize that the same type of thing would be very desirable in math. I happen to know that in your building from your third grade on up you have some kind of modified plan for reading whereby the children change rooms. Now this is similar to our school. We have nongrading in reading and we shift children among the rooms so they can read on their own level. Of course, we also do it in math, but this is in the classroom. If you are going to change for reading, why couldn't the teacher have at least several math groups so that children who are a little bit better than the rest or below average could work in math at their own level?"

Principal: "We know some teachers have been thinking about that. However, in talking with our superintendent he felt if we attack one area at a time and do it thoroughly, we would be much better off. Now of course he has had a great deal of experience with the public and with teachers and his thinking is cautious and thorough."

Dr. N: "Yes. I don't think he had too much experience with education. I happen to know that he has been in this district for about thirty years and he was the principal of the high school. I really question his knowledge and his interest in elementary education in this modern era."

Principal: "Well, of course he has a broad field. He sees things from his position and it's true that he relies heavily upon the principals in some areas. However, he does pull us together and gives us some overall concepts to follow in working with parents. Now, of course this doesn't help you and, as a fellow principal, I think you can understand this problem is a little different. Let me ask you another question. Have you talked to the teacher about your concern with this mathematics problem?"

Dr. N: "Well as you know, since you don't have regularly scheduled conferences, you do on your report card have a little box which the parent can check if he wants to have a conference with the teacher, and during the second grading period, we received the report card for our boy which was excellent. We were happy with his progress, but my wife checked the appropriate box which would indicate she should be called by the teacher to set up a conference. The teacher never called her. Apparently, she had never looked at the card. However, the thing that disturbed me a little bit about the teacher since we are still talking about the report card is that there is a space for comments on the card. I get the feeling the teacher is a very cold and aloof individual. On the report card in the space where it says 'teacher's comment,' she made a remark, 'please have all books covered.' I felt this was a little bit inappropriate on a report card."

Principal: "Would you have suggested that she send a special note home to have the books covered?"

Dr. N: "Definitely!"

Principal: "You are not objecting to her asking the books be covered, but what you are saying is, could it be on a different form or at a different time."

Dr. N: "I don't think it should be part of a permanent record."

Principal: "I see."

Dr. N: "Poor taste, frankly."

Principal: "I see."

Dr. N: "You asked about the conference. My wife did have a conference with her finally; along towards the time when she was making out the third report card. Apparently, she did see that my wife had checked the box after the second report card and, at that time, called my wife to set up an appointment. My wife went in to talk with her and she got the feeling that she was a rather cold type of individual, plus the fact she indicated our child had such good ability in math but didn't seem to be aware that we were concerned. Since my wife probably didn't know how to pursue the math problem as well as I could, I doubt if the teacher got the message as to our feeling that the child should be stimulated in math. He shouldn't sit there with the usual boredom doing the simple problems that all the class works on."

Principal: "I see. Alright, I certainly can check this out with the teacher and I can find out what the problem is, and certainly if I can help your child, I will. I must come back to our superintendent. We have talked about the possibility of developing some kind of group activity in mathematics and hopefully our superintendent will give us the green light—once he feels that the reading program is so well defined that he can go to another area. As you know, an administrator doesn't like to open two areas at the same time."

Dr. N: "It sounds to me like this is something that any good teacher and any school system would certainly have the academic freedom to pursue, especially in the skill subjects. Good teachers for ages have practiced ability grouping in both reading and math. Some teachers do it in spelling and it would just seem to me that it shouldn't call for a special unified effort unless it were to be a part of a nongrading scheme. This certainly wouldn't be a threat to the superintendent. I just can't understand how this type of thing should be such a big deal!"

Principal: "Well, I will speak with the teacher and I do appreciate as a fellow professional your comments. You had mentioned about the report card. Were you pleased with the other ways that the teacher handled this conference?"

Dr. N: "In general, yes. The rest of the conference was alright. My wife simply wanted to know how our boy was doing. She found that he was doing alright in all of the subject areas. I don't really go along with the kinds of grades that you have on the report card. For example, this is the first time that I have ever seen an A-plus on a report card and I think the division between an A-plus and an A would certainly be a hard thing to measure."

Principal: "Well, of course our superintendent believes in excellence and he felt strongly from the beginning that an A was not sufficient for some students who were doing so very well. Also we have an A-minus and he felt too that an A-minus would possibly be a little better than a B-plus but a little less than an A, and although you and I may agree as principals that it would be quite difficult for the teacher to slice things so finely, our superintendent is interested in a real professional job being done by the teacher. You may be a little surprised when I tell you, but he does call up each principal before the report cards go out and he asks us each and every time whether there were any report cards that had an unusual comment on them. We read these to him. Now that's the kind of person he is, and the kind of concern he has for education."

Dr. N: "You mean that he would support such a comment as, 'please have all books covered'?"

Principal: "Well, I don't think he would be concerned about that. He would be concerned if the teacher, let's say, misspelled some of the words in the comment column. He is very, very particular in how the cards look and the impression that the parents get. Now you are an unusual parent because you're a professional person and a principal to boot. Generally, we don't have that number of very professional people and I am sure that the superintendent would be very interested in my helping you and working with the teacher so we could reach some understanding. Let's get back to the conference if you will for a moment. Did you call the teacher or did she ask for you to come in on this conference? How was it initiated?"

Dr. N: "I had indicated my wife had checked the box after the second marking period and the teacher didn't see it until she started the report cards for the third grading period at which time she gave us a phone call and set up a conference. My wife came in one day after school and the teacher was able to give her a few minutes and sit down and talk with her."

Principal: "I see. Of course you intimated another very interesting thought; namely, that we don't have regular conference periods with parents or as regularly as some other school systems do. Our approach here is that we certainly want parents to feel comfortable in coming in to talk with us, but generally the teacher feels that if there isn't a problem, it isn't really necessary to come in. Now I don't know if you would feel comfortable with that."

Dr. N: "Well, I really believe from my own experiences that the parent-teacher conferences are a valuable way to improve communications, and I think probably most school systems will come to that eventually—even your school system. Of course, you've come halfway because at least you don't close the door on parent-teacher conferences. I would have seen the teacher myself, but I feel my being a principal might have made her a little bit ill at ease, and I feel even now as if I'm going over her head. I don't want to leave the impression that I'm coming to you over her head because you know how we principals hate people who try to pull rank; it isn't my purpose at all. It's simply to indicate to you a concern of mine and, frankly, for the betterment of all education with boys and girls rather than just my particular child."

Principal: "One of the things that I was very impressed with is the way the teacher handles the reading program. How does your boy do in reading?"

Dr. N: "Very well."

Principal: "Good."

Dr. N: "We have no problems there. We feel he is interested in reading. He, of course, has a chance to read on his level because he goes to a different classroom with some of the other very able students. The teacher surprisingly enough is rather contemporary in some of her viewpoints for she has the children pursue research projects in social studies and she encourages experiments in science. She seems to be up to date in all areas except math. If she would only allow the children to move at their own interest levels, but I guess women teachers have traditionally been a little bit weak in math. Our colleges have been a little bit weak in math education programs; since this is an interest of mine it has really been a real concern. The fact that a child can have great ability and never get the chance to blossom is personally frustrating."

Principal: "Well, we found in our school that if a parent has a specific interest in one of the subject areas it very often is found in the child and I think the teacher would be interested in knowing this; then, of course, she would want to help the child further. It is unfortunate that we don't have the kind of parent conferencing that some of the neighboring school districts have which are on a more regular basis. Our superintendent, once again, doesn't want to open too many things up at one time. He is a very careful, thoughtful person and he will plan one thing at a time and go from one activity to another. In many ways he is a bit of a perfectionist."

Dr. N: "I think he lives in the dark ages himself."

Principal: "Well, you really don't know him."

Dr. N: "I know, I don't want to say anything about your boss. I know it's your job to defend him but it kind of makes me smile a little bit."

Principal: "Well, of course, he has had a difficult job here and there have been times when the public has been less than kind to him. They haven't recognized his talent as much as they should have. Of course, you mentioned the modified Joplin plan. He was in agreement with some of the administrators who initiated this program. He certainly encouraged some of the administrators and the teachers to try this, and as teachers and administrators came up with new ideas, he helped them if they planned carefully. But here again he is not like some educators who will go into new programs haphazardly. He does think things out. This is true and I guess it seems to some that he is less than able."

Dr. N: "I tend to feel that the kind of real changes that affect the entire school system for the good of all will not take place as long as he is on the scene. Yet within a person's own building I would certainly feel that there would be some good chances for the encouragement of individual teachers to do the kind of grouping and work that would benefit children."

Principal: "Well, I agree with you. I think also that we work as a system and that we work within the organization. The superintendent sets the tone. He deems it necessary to work in the area of reading within this modified Joplin plan. We will go along and certainly be very supportive of him. However, you do have some good ideas and I think maybe as we go on, we will be getting into the area of mathematics. Maybe we will be doing more with individualization in other areas. What other things can I help you and your boy with and pass on to the teacher in a nice way so that she knows you have some of these concerns?"

Dr. N: "It's only the math that bothers me and I can't understand that if the teacher is going to be creative in all other areas of the curriculum, why it is that the math part of it has to be held back. I certainly think that if she were given encouragement and support from above in taking students beyond the math curriculum for their grade she would do so. I would certainly think any good teacher, especially if she goes in this direction in other subject areas, would take the hint."

Principal: "Of course, you are talking about going beyond the grade level work. I think you are very aware of the fact that you are talking about a very typical grade level that this teacher has been trained in and is skilled in. Your boy is in this grade level. Now, are you saying the teacher should do more and go into another grade over and above what the designation on the door reads?"

Dr. N: "Well I really don't think that a fourth grade teacher is locked by experience and training into a fourth grade classroom. I cerainly think she would have the ability to take a child into fifth grade math if the situation warranted, and frankly I wouldn't have a teacher on my staff who didn't have that ability. I would want each teacher to be confident in moving any of my fourth grade students into fifth grade math work when the students showed that they were ready."

Principal: "Well, let me ask you a question then. Suppose we had a hypothetical case—what would the fifth grade teacher in my school say if your boy, when he goes into her class, knows all the lessons? How would she feel about this?"

Dr. N: "Frankly, that would be her problem. In September she would take the child where he is and move him beyond that point. I don't see why a child should be held back."

Principal: "Of course, you have an interesting approach, and I have heard of this before. I have read some of the professional journals and they refer to a number of changes in education and I think it has interest. I don't think our district is thinking in that vein. However, I would be delighted to . . ."

Dr. N: "Delighted to keep thinking in that vein . . . I would hope."

Principal: "No, not necessarily. I think it's good to open windows and let new ideas in. I think at this point we are talking about a grade level situation. I know some of the teachers and I think that the teacher your boy has might be very uncomfortable if the fifth grade teacher would then say to her, 'You taught this boy fifth grade work. What am I going to teach him?' Now I know you are going to say that the child should be continued from that point, but you see, we are not thinking in that way."

Dr. N: "That's the part that bothers me frankly, and I can say from experience that when teachers are exposed to taking children as far as they are able to go in all subject areas, although some teachers might be a little hesitant and may resist a little bit at first, you will find beyond that point they will endorse the idea fully."

Principal: "Was there anything else you were concerned about?"

Dr. N: "Not concerned, just curious. Why do children seldom go out-doors even when the weather is nice? I have spoken to my son and he states that even in the spring months, physical education classes are conducted in the gymnasium."

Principal: "Well, actually some of our teachers prefer not to take children outside. You know there is a greater chance for accidents on the playground. Besides, teachers know that children get an opportunity to play outside once they go home from school."

Mr. N: "Oh, do teachers decide that physical education classes will be held indoors?"

Principal: "Not exactly. In my school I lean heavily on teacher judgment. I trust the professionalism of the staff."

Dr. N: "It's interesting that you mention teacher judgment. My wife was very concerned earlier in the year when she found that during released time for religious training, the students who remained in the room were unsupervised for long periods of time while the classroom teacher took coffee breaks. I understand that until several mothers complained, this condition went unnoticed by the administration."

Principal: "That was a most embarrassing situation. When I found out, I called a meeting of the entire staff and we worked out a rotating method where teachers could have a coffee break and still have some coverage for the classes during released time."

Dr. N: "I understood that most schools take advantage of released time and do review work on a one-to-one basis with the remaining students."

Principal: "Well thank you for coming in to see me. I'll follow up your concern."

1. Does the building principal answer Dr. N, the parent, satisfactorily?

2. If you were the teacher, would you have done anything different with Dr. N's son?

3. Does the building principal have a point when he states, "What would the fifth grade teacher in my school say if your boy, when he goes into her class, knows all the lessons? How would she feel about this?"

4. What impressions does this case study give you of the school superintendent?

5. Does the public school have the responsibility of taking the student as far as it can in one year or does the one grade at a time approach fit better into the school pattern?

The dilemma that Dr. N finds himself in is unfortunately common in educational circles today.

An over-cautious superintendent who obviously is holding the reins very tightly not only inhibits progress but crushes creative thinking on the part of his principals and teachers. The principal states to Dr. N, "We have talked about the possibility of developing some kind of group activity in mathematics and hopefully our superintendent will give us the green light once he feels that the reading program is so well defined that he can go to another area.

As you know, an administrator doesn't like to open two areas at the same time."

Dr. N raises an interesting point about academic freedom for the professional schoolman and he states, "This certainly wouldn't be a threat to the superintendent."

Dr. N and the building principal find themselves miles apart when, after the parent speaks about teaching children on their own level, the building principal states, "Well, of course our superintendent believes in excellence and he felt very strongly from the beginning that an A was not sufficient for some students who were doing so very well. Also we have an A-minus and he felt too that an A-minus would possibly be a little better than a B-plus but a little less than an A."

This kind of lint-picking thinking is still prevalent in education and Dr. N's comment is pertinent: "I tend to feel that the kind of real changes that affect the entire school system for the good of all will not take place as long as he is on the scene."

Real positive change comes to school communities from an enlightened public who through their elected boards of education hire superintendents who encourage creative schoolmanship.

CHAPTER SEVENTEEN

Where Have We Gone Wrong?

In the case described in this chapter, Joan, who has had all the advantages of a comfortable middle-class home, dislikes school and is likely to drop out. The question throughout this conference is, could anything have been done before junior high school to help Joan?

How many Joans do we have in the elementary school who are of above-average intelligence and yet have not been properly motivated? How do principals identify Joans early enough when teachers have classes of thirty and more children?

Do the junior high schools have a responsibility in contacting parents early in the beginning years?

The elementary supervisor states the problem in these words: "to recognize that children have different learning styles, and I think probably the hardest thing for us is really to determine what a child's learning style is and to learn how to teach children according to their own style."

Is there a need to take a hard look at what educators are doing to children? Do teachers teach to the average child and let the extremes in a class, the very able and the slow, fall by the wayside?

Since these and other questions go largely unanswered today, it is appropriated that we study this case which focuses on the real concerns of a mother who is desperately worried about her child's not adjusting to the public schools.

Case no. 71P
Principal: "Good morning Mrs. P. It's very nice to see you again.

We haven't seen you since Joan left our school. How are things going?"

Mrs. P: "I'm afraid not as well as I would like them to. That is the reason why I am here."

Principal: "Oh, what can we do for you?"

Mrs. P: "Well, I have a lot of questions. Just what kind of communication goes on between the elementary school and the junior high—for instance, when it comes to placing a child in his proper program, let's say for the seventh grade?"

Principal: "I see. What class is Joan in now?"

Mrs. P: "She is in the ninth grade."

Principal: "She has gone through the seventh, eighth and now is in the ninth grade. I see. Well, Miss R, our supervisor, can tell us a few things about how our sixth grade teachers place children and maybe we can take it from there."

Miss R: "Each year, the junior high school guidance department sends us forms which we complete for each of our sixth graders. These forms require information on children's achievement testing and ability testing, as well as on the achievement of the child in the classroom. There is also a place for teacher's comments and teacher's recommendations. Each teacher also meets with the guidance counselor for a short time so that they can share some information, and from that point the guidance department of the junior high school takes over in placing the children who feed into the seventh grade."

Mrs. P: "Well, might I ask, when a sixth grade teacher makes a recommendation to the guidance counselor of a secondary school, don't they act upon it favorably? What is the point of the teacher making a recommendation?"

Miss R: "That is a good question and a hard one to answer. I would assume there are a number of factors the junior high school has to take into account. It's difficult because of limited schedules and class space and perhaps because they set up other criteria that may be, to their way of thinking, more important than teacher recommendation or teacher judgment."

Mrs. P: "Now is the California test an achievement test or an I.Q. test?"

Miss R: "It's a test of mental maturity when you say I.Q."

Mrs. P: "What happens to a child who achieves very well in a test such as this? She does about as well as you can but achieves fairly average scores on these achievement tests. It seems to me after putting a child in a so-called average class based on achievement, wouldn't it be a good idea if they tried another tack? Perhaps put a child in a better-than-average class in the hope that the child will be stimulated by a more advanced kind of work. I don't know exactly what to call it. If you rule out emotional difficulty of any sort or anything like that, why isn't the child functioning?"

Miss R: "Are you talking about the junior high school or elementary school or both?"

Mrs. P: "Well, both possibly, because this is now affecting her on a secondary level. Of course, I would like any future generation to avoid this sort of thing if possible."

Miss R: "I think one of the things that we at the elementary level are trying very hard to keep up with is checking where we see a great discrepancy between achievement and ability. Very often tests, particularly the kind of group tests we give, are not as accurate as they could be, but when we do spot this kind of discrepancy it is our responsibility to look into it and, as you say, rule out emotional factors and physical problems that might cause it. As a matter of fact, one of the things we have learned recently about very young children is that theirs is an area which is completely unexplored in terms of perceptual difficulty. It has come about because we have discovered young children who are not learning to read and yet have the ability to read and, as we find out more about children, we discover more about why they learn in certain ways. This has opened up a completely new field to all of us in education."

Mrs. P: "But, of course, speaking personally since I know there isn't any emotional factor or any physical difficulty for I have had all these tested more than once, it is very difficult for me to understand why my child is achieving just about as low as she can. She just barely passes practically all of her subjects. With what I've been told—a very high I.Q. and a great deal of ability—I cannot understand why she is constantly being placed in an average or low average class. In other words no one has bothered to look at her ability. All they are doing is looking at her class-work marks, which obviously are not an adequate reflection of her. She is not learning in class and while I hate to be the kind of a mother who says 'my child is bored,' this is the only word I can use. I never approved of people saying this, but of course I know we are all a little prejudiced. I've been informed many times that she has superior ability and she is barely doing well, with what they call a mere 70% average in all her secondary school work. It's beyond me to understand why she isn't functioning any better."

Principal: "I think we may be in the area of motivation and interest. It seems to me if she has a high I.Q. and she has scored very well on these tests and yet her achievement scores are low and these other areas have been checked out as you say, we should look into the area of motivation and interest. Now how does she feel about school? Does she talk about some of the teachers or subjects with interest, excitement and enthusiasm or is she just rather neutral about it?"

Mrs. P: "I would say that she's going to school and just marking time. I feel she is accomplishing nothing. She goes to school with no enthusiasm whatsoever; with the exception of two teachers she happened to have last term, I have never heard her speak really favorably about anyone. She happened to come in contact with a teacher this year and she has asked to be in one of his classes next year because he's very impressed with her. But she hasn't been in any of his classes yet. This is the only enthusiasm I have seen her show at all in many years. As I said, I would like to know, how do you motivate?"

Miss R: "Well, I think this is another—and again I don't want to sound as if we are passing the buck—but again this is a new kind of thing for many of us in education; not only to take into account achievement and ability, but to recognize that children have different learning styles, and I think probably the hardest thing for us is really to determine what a child's learning style is and to learn how to teach children according to their own style. We are finding that certain children learn better by themselves. You know, just give them things and put them off in a corner and they really don't need much else. Some children learn visually and some children learn kinesthetically. So these areas again are new to us and it's unfortunate Joan isn't starting elementary school now. As you say, you're thinking about children. You know for the future years it isn't just Joan that you're concerned with. There is hope that some of these children are going to change; that children who have ability will be challenged in ways that they never have been challenged before because very often bright children are just bored or disinterested or seem to be daydreaming because they are so far ahead of what's going on around them."

Principal: "Miss R mentioned before a case in our school here on the elementary level, where the teacher is trying to reach a child using unusual methods and she has been quite successful. Now maybe you would like to take a minute and mention some of these techniques, because I was fascinated by them myself, and I wonder sometimes if we as teachers don't tend to be too rigid as we work with kids, possibly not taking into account the different learning styles that children have."

Miss R: "This case is probably parallel to Joan's in some way. This is a young boy who also came from New York city and had been accelerated in the city's schools. When he first came to us, a judgment was made that he was not achieving at the same level as the other children and he has been with us now for three years. We have not been terribly successful in motivating him. This year the teacher who has him has taken kindly to the idea of just leaving him alone; not neglecting him but letting him seek his way of learning and giving him things to work with. She has given him assignments but not the same kind of assignments, not at the same rate, not in the same way the other children are learning, and he is doing a great job."

Mrs. P: "I would say this might hold true for Joan. When she has been given an assignment—research work to do or book reports to do—she comes out with fabulous marks and all kinds of good remarks by the teacher on the project, but this is the only good mark she gets. It is only the sort of thing that she cannot go off and do research on that she has trouble with. I remember her telling me last term that one of her teachers was out sick a few weeks and they had a substitute. Joan took scads of notes and enjoyed having the substitute. She enjoyed that whole block of time, two weeks or whatever it was that her regular teacher was out. I have not heard since the regular teacher came back that she was enjoying the subject at all; so obviously this is true and I did hear somewhere that the elementary schools, and I should hope the secondary schools, will try to do more individualized work. Is this the correct term to use?"

Miss R: "Yes, I think the word individualization in itself means individual children first at the rate they learn, in the style they learn, and the way they learn. We recognize more and more that there are differences in children and the problem is the time and the amount of skill it takes to truly individualize with large classes and with some of the other limitations that have been placed upon us. I think now we are finally at the point maybe where we know more than we have the facility to do with. There was a time when we had lots of things and we didn't know what to do with them. Now we know what to do with a lot of things and we don't have enough materials and working tools. So much research is being done now and there is so much we can do if we only had the know-how."

Mrs. P: "I had a terrible thing against guidance counselors until this year. I must say that about two months ago I finally found a guidance counselor who might know what's going on. The one she had for two years before this was useless. He used only the most negative kind of remarks and, based on these sort of remarks, I can only assume that he never once looked into her folder. When I asked him last year why she was flunking, he said to me, 'Mrs. P, I see no evidence of your daughter's superior ability.' Now I know this is a bunch of hogwash because I have been told ever since she started school including when she was in elementary school that her I.Q. range was anywhere between 135 and 140 and I hardly think that this is an average or below-average child. I personally think this shows superior ability. Now if he bothered to look into her records I know information is there because they came from the city that way and since she was tested and I got results, I don't know how he possibly could have made a remark like that. The only thing I can construe is that they are not looking at the children's ability at all and they are simply going on what children accomplish in the classroom. I'd like to know how you go about helping a child like this, since I have had her to a psychologist? She is physically well. What do I do now? And what could anybody do with their own child who might run into this difficulty?"

Miss R: "Well, I have had experience personally with guidance counselors and my feeling is that they base many of their judgments on test scores. They do have tests that they give students in secondary schools. Whether they look at the earlier test scores I would almost doubt, but I know that they do test them in the junior high school and that they do use those scores quite heavily.

I had a similar concern when I went to the high school guidance counselor because the school refused my child placement in
the accelerated program—his entrance test score was one percentile
below the cutoff point. I feel that they rely too heavily on test scores
in making judgments. They aren't looking at the child or the child's
ability; so I think we all have our own problems. I think when we
deal with large numbers of children, we set very strict rules on what
can or cannot be done. I think one of the things, at least our elementary school is trying very hard to do is be more flexible and to
make exceptions. Certainly we have to set criteria. We have to say
students should pass this or should be able to accomplish 85%
before they can go on to the next area or whatever, and we do have
to set standards because we cannot operate without them. But they
also have to be flexible. We have to be able to look at a child and
say, well I know this child doesn't test well or this child doesn't function well in this situation but he has the ability and so we give him
the opportunity to be challenged. We are human."

Mrs. P: "Yes, of course. This leads me to something which I
have contemplated, but I don't know whether it's worthwhile. The
classes in the public schools are as large as they are and I understand you do have in each class five children or maybe ten who need
special help. I have contemplated many times taking my daughter
out of public school and putting her in private school. I am not
sure this is the answer any more either because I don't know what
effect this would have on her personality. She again may feel like
a failure because she does feel like one now. She has a very poor
image of herself because she is constantly being told 'you really
should be in better classes but you don't deserve it.' And really if
this doesn't work after five, six or seven years, isn't it time somebody said something nice to her? I must say that last term, the
reason my daughter reacted well to two teachers was because they
did say something nice to her. She did an autobiography and the
teacher said, 'What a delight it was to read and what a delight it
is to have you in my class!' Now this is a nice thing to say to a
child. She got a good mark on the autobiography. It was very large
and she had a tremendous number of things to say about herself.
The teacher enjoyed it obviously. She didn't really have to say anything nice, but this is one of the first times this child has heard a
pleasant thing said to her in seven years of school. They say she's

a pleasant child; she never gets into any trouble. This is hardly a thing to say to someone who is already 15 years old. It's time to say something different to her because it's having a negative effect on her. She knows that she's being put into average or below-average classes. In fact last term, because it was only an average English class, hers wasn't permitted to go to the Shakespeare Festival. Now, this doesn't make any sense to me. What are the criteria for taking an honors class to a Shakespeare Festival? I don't think this is a right thing to do. Where are the criteria here? Why is one class permitted to go and not everyone? I think sometimes in your average or low-average classes, a lot of the children who are in those classes have never been to a Shakespeare Festival and I think they might benefit from going. I just don't understand how they operate. I think I've had sleepless nights trying to figure these things out and what to do."

Principal: "One of the things that concern me, and Mrs. P brought this up, is the problem of self-image; Miss R and I have talked quite a bit about that in our school in terms of the importance of the self-image of the child and how the teacher works with the child. I would wonder if maybe Joan doesn't project a feeling of the kind of self-image that she wants. Obviously, she doesn't feel too good about school. Maybe if you continue to work with the guidance counselor at the junior high you could talk about this, because we know this is very important. What are some of the things you've done, Miss R, with this?"

Miss R: "Well, a thought went through my head having a child in college already and having gone through this. I almost feel sorry because it seems to me if the elementary school doesn't succeed in building a positive self-image for a child, the chances are very slight along the way that something is going to happen, because once the child leaves the elementary school it is unusual to find teachers really interested in children. They expect that children come to them prepared to take the thing that they have to give in a mature way and they give it to them in a take-it-or-leave-it fashion. It's an unusual secondary teacher who can do personal things for children. They do see 140 children a day. They do have heavy schedules. They do have papers to do and other things, and they do not have the time to develop the kind of relationship with a child that an elementary school teacher has. I think the responsibility is really ours in the elementary school to develop children with a positive self-image, a love for school, a love for learning and some very basic skills on how to learn things. I think maybe this is something a lot of children just don't have by the time they get to junior high. They haven't learned yet how to accept what teachers are going to give them."

Mrs. P: "You see, I said this term I felt her guidance counselor has touched one little thing which encourages me and I can hardly wait for this term to be over and next term to begin because I keep hoping this is going to help her a little bit. They took some sort of a test. I don't know what sort of test it was, but when I went in to the guidance counselor, he showed me that she scored at the 98th percentile on anything to do with verbal ability and at the 23rd percentile in math. I hope they encourage the good things that happen somewhere along the way, although I am beginning to think it's too late. The other things might come along a little bit better then because she will be more comfortable with them. Her math teacher told me, as a matter of fact, she's already dropped her for the term. I realize she is going to have to repeat it in order to graduate. The teacher said the minute she calls on Joan she doesn't even stop to think whether she knows the answer. She immediately says, I don't know. However, I started to say that the guidance counselor is going to put her in an honors English class next term in spite of the fact that her class marks don't warrant it. The mere fact that she did have a 98th percentile on this test should place her in an honors class. But you see this is the thing I've been talking about all this time and nobody believed me. I couldn't say to them, 'You are not looking at the child.' As a matter of fact, she received commendations from the press for two articles she had in a juvenile magazine. Nobody ever thought about telling anyone about it. The fact that she writes well should be encouraged in some way. Now again I don't know how this could be. Frankly her spelling and her grammar leave a great deal to be desired, but if this is all English and English classes are based on . . . Of course, when she takes a test in English and grammar, she fails terribly on it, so it pulls down her other marks; can't this be taken into consideration in some way?"

Principal: "One of the things we are trying to do, and Miss R and I are both on a committee working with the junior high school

English department, is to articulate better with them. We feel when our children go to junior high, there should be enough flexibility so that children may be placed on many different levels and be given many different opportunities. We would agree with you that sometimes test scores aren't true indications of how children will perform in the next few years. Some children develop later. Different kinds of learning stimuli affect different children. Sometimes, as Miss R said, different teaching techniques are needed like the one which is being used by one of our teachers where she lets the child work at his own rate and level. If he wants to do arithmetic during the English period, he may and if he wants to do science during the spelling period, he may. Although this takes a much different kind of teacher, and I might add a very understanding parent to go with it, it's something that we are now experimenting with. Hopefully as we work with the junior high, we are developing more flexibility. Do you want to comment on this, Miss R, because parents are very concerned about placement and what happens to our children as they do get into junior high?"

Miss R: "I think the committee we worked on helped us a little bit and it's going to be a long, hard pull before seeing eye to eye, and frankly I don't know if we ever will. Maybe it's too much to expect. Maybe we're going to have to learn to live with each other and to transfer some of our thinking to each other. Maybe we don't understand what they are trying to say. But in elementary school, it's child-centered and in secondary it's subject-centered and there is a big difference between the two. However, we have met and of course the emphasis was on our nongraded program which has thrown some areas into confusion at the junior high school. Some of our children have been exposed to things even the advanced junior high school seventh grade classes thought were in their curriculum so they had a little bit of a revolution this year and it started something going. Now this is what has come from it—a discussion, a dialogue and some understanding of what we are trying to do with children in the elementary level and where the junior high school can pick up from that point. They still want us to do certain things. You know it's always passed down. As a matter of fact, I think it's probably the first time the sixth grade teachers are meeting with the chairmen of the departments of the junior high school. They will attempt to carry this dialogue further so that they can get a better understanding of what the sixth grade teacher thinks about his children. Perhaps, we can do a little bit more in the elementary school to prepare our children for the things they are going to face in the junior high and maybe the junior high will better understand what we are trying to do and what kind of child we are giving to them."

Mrs. P: "It seems to me I do understand a secondary school has to be more subject-oriented, but a school is not in existence except for children and, therefore, they are losing the whole point of why the kids are going to school. My daughter is losing the whole point of going to school and if I could find something better to do with her, I honestly think she would be happier not to be in school. She looks for excuses to stay home."

Miss R: "I wonder if this isn't also part of our changing society. I think maybe even five or ten years ago kids did not question things. You went to school. You were expected to do so many pages of arithmetic and so many of English and you wrote your spelling words five times each. Whether you hated it or not you had to do it, you did it and you didn't dare tell anybody you didn't like it. I think today with the kind of children we have—they're making us sensitive to what they really think and what they really feel and maybe they have felt all along that we didn't know about things. Perhaps, with Joan because she is an unusual child you knew about it sooner, but I think many children feel this way. Today kids are a lot more verbal and are exposed to many more things and hear about many more things. They are telling us what they do or don't like, in their own way, sometimes through demonstrating and sometimes they are just failing. They are doing it in their own special way."

Mrs. P: "I often wondered if I had been told, perhaps when she was much younger, that they felt she might do better in a private school—maybe she didn't get the right attention—the sort of attention she personally needed. I am not blaming anyone. I realize it's impossible when you have 30 children in a classroom, where probably in a class there are five or six or even ten children who need speical help it becomes quite a job. I wonder if she might have been better off all this time in private school. I don't know whether the public school would ever say to a parent, 'Maybe your child should be in private school.' I had contemplated this all along since

I was told when she was very young in kindergarten that she was extremely bright. I am constantly being told this even today when an adult comes in contact with her. They will always say to me, 'How old is she?' I have had this when she was eight, when she was ten and now that she is going on fifteen. I am constantly being told this again. They are always amazed that she is as young as she is, but I never knew what to do. Would I be hurting her socially? Was I going to put her down, using her own expression, by taking her out of public school because she wasn't functioning properly? Because she was told she wasn't doing the things she should be doing, not by myself, but by her teachers? She has constantly had negative things said to her. I would have taken her out of public school and put her in private school if I felt it would help. I am just a mother and I figured these people know better. Then if someone would have suggested it, perhaps I would have done it."

Miss R: "Because there are only five or six children in the classroom doesn't necessarily mean there will be a better situation. If you had all the facility and all the know-how to find the school, you might find one that would be suited for her and it might have been the best thing if it was what she needed."

Mrs. P: "Of course, she doesn't have too much time left in school, but it's still disturbing to know this child has to start looking for colleges in two years; and with the marks that she has I really don't know what I'm going to do."

Miss R: "Well, I wonder if high school isn't going to be a better situation than the junior high school is. I think perhaps in high school sometimes, there is an opportunity for some of the honors courses. There is the opportunity to be challenged in the area where the student is the strongest. I think too, both you and she and everybody is going to have to recognize in which area she is strong and in which area she isn't, and whether she's in high school or college, she may never be a math student."

Mrs. P: "Yes, I appreciate this."

Miss R: "And we all learn to live with it."

Mrs. P: "Right."

Miss R: "If English or social studies is her forte, then by getting involved in those areas, in clubs and other activities and getting to meet some of the teachers who have more skills and recognize children for what they're worth other than the assignments they complete, then maybe she will suddenly find her place."

Mrs. P: "I keep hoping that this day will come. I don't think I have any further questions."

Principal: "Let me tell you what I would suggest because I think we have covered some important points. I would suggest that you see how the high school experience is and, as Miss R said, maybe this will open up new doors for her; if she doesn't do well after the first year in high school, it might be a very good idea to meet with the guidance counselor and ask for a series of diagnostic tests and suggestions about what can be done. You may then want to come to a decision about whether the last few years of high school should be spent in private school or whether to request a change in some of her courses. I know you are interested in having Joan go to college and I would think after the first year in high school, it may be well to look into this."

Miss R: "Well, I think that you can only tell with time. If college is the goal, and unfortunately a fact of life today is that colleges look at scores, you might investigate colleges that use different criteria for entrance and see what kind of things they offer youngsters. There are such schools and it would certainly be wise to be very close to this guidance counselor whom you feel so comfortable with. I think, as parents of young children, we tend to be much more involved with the school. We come to school more often. We are invited more often and tend to take a more active role. But as secondary parents, we are invited once a year and we tend to stay in the background until something very drastic happens. I really think it's our responsibility as parents to be a little more involved, particularly if we feel we have a real concern. I think that once they get to know you or anyone else and realize that you have a realistic feeling about your child and a real concern then they are cooperative. I know that I've had that experience with the guidance counselor at the high school and was very pleased with his attitude and his interest. I felt my child was no longer a number or a name to him."

Mrs. P: "You would be interested to know that my daughter is terribly interested in psychology at this stage of the game. Of course, she cannot understand why if she wants to be a psychiatrist and deal with people that she has to have math courses."

Miss R: "Tell her research studies require a math background. Tell her to come talk to me. I was a psychology major."

Mrs. P: "I can't figure her out. The guidance counselor spoke to her. She said, 'Joan, the way your marks are you may have difficulty getting into the college you like. If so, why don't you consider our community college for the first two years and maybe your marks will pick up. Maybe you could go to a different school after that.' But Joan's reaction was, only dumb kids go to a community college because they can't get into any other school. However, her guidance counselor told me that she would show her the names of children who have gone through community college, who are honor students and for one reason or another went there anyway, whether it be lack of finances or the parents or whatever. But you see it's being circulated around the neighborhood that the kids that go to community college are stupid."

Miss R: "Well, that's the kind of thing that happens now. But you have to live through it; once the kids are actually involved and get to work they find out differently. It's hard. It really is hard to counteract their peers' reactions and those generalizations, 'only this kind of kid goes there.' But maturity takes care of a lot of them and they learn that there are kids at community college who just don't want to leave home. They could go anywhere they want to. They just don't want to. It's realistic now to think about and investigate other schools. As I said, I am sure there are schools where academic achievement is not the sole criterion."

Mrs. P: "Of course, being the kind of kid she is, she doesn't tend to volunteer for too many things because her feelings are negative. She went to see a play at school and I asked her who some of the kids are in it and she said, 'Well, who did you expect?' and rattled off the same kids who are in all the plays. And I said, 'Did you ever think of going in and trying out for it?' Well, she did once when she was in the seventh grade, and because she didn't get any part, she'll never do it again. She said the whole thing is cliquish and it's always the same kids. I agree, it's always the same kids. I try to make her understand it's probably because they're the only kids who volunteer. But again, the whole thing about school is negative. I have been trying to change it. In fact now I have gotten to a point where I have hardly even mentioned school to her because I am tired of making a thing over it. I am trying to ignore it, but I don't know if this is healthy."

Miss R: "I know very often people, teen-agers especially, would like to be what they aren't. They think they would like to be the most popular girl in the class or the hero, and they aren't, and it takes them a little time to appreciate themselves for what they are. I think high school is that kind of time where everybody would like to be the most popular girl or boy in the class, but also there is something about accepting yourself, and saying I am just never going to be the most popular kid. I am never going to be the one who gets the lead role, but I have other qualities. Now it would have been great if these things had come from other places till now, but they haven't and so now that she is getting older, she has to begin to accept herself for what she is, and for what she has and for what she doesn't have."

Mrs. P: "You see this is one of the reasons I have felt all along, and this goes back to being constantly told 'you should be achieving more and you're not,' that her self-image has been damaged. Someone who hasn't a self-image may say, 'big deal—let those kids get involved with the show. So I can't act or I don't look good on the stage or whatever is used as a criterion for these kids having gotten the part.' But again, she has a poor self-image and she naturally tends to blame other people, of course. I understand this. I think we all do this."

Miss R: "Have patience."

Mrs. P: "Faith is what I'm trying very hard to have, but you know it becomes a little more difficult each year because things get worse instead of better. Anyway, because she dropped from what was at least a mid 80% average last year, I dread seeing her final report card because I'll bet she doesn't have better than a 70% or maybe a 75% average. I think it's dreadful with a child's ability like this."

Principal: "I think it's a shame that we put such emphasis on marks. One of the purposes in a nongraded program is to think in terms of the individual child and his ability to work rather than in terms of grades. What I suggest of course is that you continue to give support to Joan and continue to work on her self-image. Especially, as Miss R said, being a girl and a teen-ager in itself brings about concerns. Then I would suggest going to the guidance counselor and seeing if we can get her in that honors English class because this would be a big boost for her ego. It may very likely open all kinds of areas to her. I would very definitely, after the first year of high school, sit down with the guidance counselor and decide where you want to go from there. Then you would have an opportunity to seek out a good private school or continue with public high school. Here the guidance department should be able to do a lot.

"Well, thank you very much for coming in. I hope this helped a little."

Mrs. P: "Good-bye."

1. Does Mrs. P, Joan's parent, have a real complaint with the public schools?
2. What should the junior high school guidance department do?
3. Is there a different approach to children on the junior high level?
4. If you were Joan's teacher, what might you do to try to motivate her?

The real frustration that faces the teacher in Joan's case is how Joan can be motivated to work up to her ability.

Joan, an only child from an upper middle-class family, has been exposed to all the benefits of an affluent, suburban way of life. She has a better than average I.Q. and yet intensely dislikes school.

Miss R, the school's elementary supervisor, suggests that possibly Joan's learning styles have not been reached and that an individualized learning experience is what she needs.

It was unfortunate that the concern of Joan's mother had not been detected by the junior high and a complete follow-up including academic and psychological tests performed.

The concern over the articulation between the elementary school and the junior high school keeps cropping up as both the parent and the supervisor allude to the apparent lack of communication.

The principal speaks about more flexibility in the schools, especially as it relates to junior high placement. The subject-centered approach which has been a secondary school approach and also at times has overshadowed the elementary school is changing as new methods are introduced on the elemenary level. As students enter junior high, having been exposed to post-elementary work in the skills areas, secondary placement will of necessity be more on an individualized basis.

CHAPTER EIGHTEEN

Give Me That

Old-time Report Card

This chapter presents the concerns of a mother whose children have brought home a different kind of report card. A parent who is familiar with A's, B's and C's now has to face S's and U's.

Many schools form committees of parents and teachers who study many different kinds of reporting systems before they recommend to the school administrators a new marking system. Many hours of meetings with parents are spent in explaining what a good evaluation system is before a school puts a new reporting system into operation.

In the final analysis, the class room teacher and the principal are the ones who make or break a reporting-to-parents system. A well-planned, carefully developed approach to a new reporting system can be successful when the teaching staff explains the system to students and parents.

In this chapter, the parent should have been informed about what the S means on the report card. Obviously she was not orientated to the change in reporting to parents.

Case no. 6C

Principal: "Good morning, Mrs. C. It's so nice to see you. May I help you this morning?"

Mrs. C: "Yes, thank you. I hope you can. I hope at least you can solve some of my problems. I know that when I come to you as a concerned parent you tell me that many of the policies are not settled here in the elementary school but are determined in the district as a whole. I know you don't always have a definite answer. But I'm particularly concerned because my children came home from school with their report cards and I can't really tell from the cards how well they've done. I have three children. All of them came home with S, S, S, S, S which means that they are doing up to expected level and as I look at all three report cards, they all look identical. I don't think the report card as such tells me enough about my children."

Principal: "Well, I am glad you mentioned this because this is one of the concerns we have been working with. Miss R, would you like to comment on that?"

Miss R: "Well, I thought your comment about your three children not being identical is a tremendous clue to why our report cards are the way they are. Perhaps a little background about the report card and the change from the traditional report card that we used at one time is in order. Our marks were 78, 80, 90, 92, 95, and then we changed to letter grade—A, B, C, D and F—and now we have done away with that and we have come to expected level of working or not working at expected level."

Mrs. C: "First, before we go any further, why did you do away with the other marks?"

Miss R: "Well, this was done, interestingly enough, for the reason you mentioned, because all children are different. What we were doing when we graded children according to a letter or a number, was saying that a child or every child could be graded in the same way and we set artificial standards. We were saying that a child had to measure up to this standard and could measure up to 90%, 70%, or 80%."

Mrs. C: "Percent of what?"

Miss R: "Of what we thought they should be doing."

Mrs. C: "Not necessarily 100% of a perfect paper or 90% or 80% of the presented material?"

Miss R: "Right! What we were saying is that we were setting up for every child and for every grade, a certain amount of material, a certain amount of learning and then we were measuring what percentage of that learning could be accomplished. Now, we realized we were basing this on a false standard because we recognized that every child in that grade was different and had a different intelligence and a different way of learning. We could not expect children to all learn the same things in the same way at the same time. Therefore, what we were doing was creating in the very beginning false standards. We were measuring children against a false standard. We were finding some children who were always failing, not because they weren't trying but because they just couldn't do better percentage-wise. They couldn't do better than sixty percent of what we said every child in fourth grade or third grade should do and we found children who were always getting 100% or 95% and yet who were not really being challenged in what they could do. There was a shade of difference all the way up and down the line."

Mrs. C: "Well for an over-achiever—if that's the word—I don't know how you could over-achieve, but for those who do well and could make hundred's and ninety's and above, then they could be given enrichment programs and still use the same material. They could just be given more. But it would seem to me that all through life you and I are going to be graded, given a position or a job. You and I could apply for the same job later in life and I could try as hard as I might, but if I don't have the skills that you have I wouldn't make it. So why is it really any different in school? Mustn't a child be prepared to accept even at a young age that life is life? I have three children and two of them are good average kids; the other is a very high achiever. I don't think it's wrong. I think it must be a stigma for a child to know that he isn't even basically as bright as another. I think you should know how you stand from the beginning of life on through, then you are better equipped to handle yourself when you compete for jobs later in life."

Miss R: "I agree with you completely and I think part of this is built into our psychology, although it may not seem obvious but we as teachers and as educators say this. Every child should be aware of what he can do—one way or the other—and should be rated or evaluated on what he can do. Now we know, going along with this, we have to tell children you cannot read the fourth grade book. You can only read the third grade book or the other book, but if you do well and work hard at it, you will excel. We are not dropping our standards nor are we dropping our expectations for children; nor are we doing away with competition because that's built in children. It's just that it's based on something else rather than a grade or mark. It's based on what you as an individual are capable of doing and reaching your potential as an individual. It's more realistic."

Mrs. C: "Well, it seems to me by looking at this report card that I can't tell your opinion as a teacher and is this not what this is? The opinion of the teacher."

Miss R: "Yes, somewhat."

Mrs. C: "What is the expected level of my child? I cannot tell by looking at the report card what that level is. I've been told that this is the purpose of the parent-teacher conference. But in my experience now, and I've had two years with this, without exception, unless I ask the teacher specific, pointed questions, she will not tell me that he is on an average with the other children his age or is on grade level. Many parents won't do this and for the first couple of conferences I wouldn't do it either. I thought what she told me was all I needed to know, but I felt when I got home that my son's and my two daughters' report cards all seemed exactly the same. I would like to know if he is a little stronger in math than he is in reading. Is he a little slower to comprehend one subject than the other? But without my asking specifically, the teacher will not tell me."

Miss R: "Well, maybe this points up something that we have to do with our report card. This is why I have been interested in studying the kinds of things that other school districts do. In many cases, they have done away with some of the symbols we have in terms of using an S or an N. Rather it's a complete comment report card where the teacher will write on the card, 'John is working well in math or he needs help in math skills; he's doing better in language arts or he writes creatively.' The comments on the report card are thus geared to telling you the kinds of things you now have to ask the teacher. This report card of ours is still only in its second year in use and probably will have to be revised so that we can get a better communication between the parent and the teacher."

Mrs. C: "If I remember correctly, the reporting system before this one not only told whether the child was or was not doing as the teacher felt he was capable, but it also told what level he was on. If I may use the word level instead of grades. Why isn't that a better system than the one we have now? I can truly understand why this system, perhaps, is better for a child because he doesn't feel a sense of failure, time after time. That I can understand, I agree with you wholeheartedly, but as a parent I don't think it tells me enough. If I was blind and I felt that my child, my son, was just terrific and this report card kept saying S, S, S in reading, S in English and he is doing up to his expected level, I would feel great. If I didn't go to the teacher and ask specifically these questions that I am concerned about, and I let him go all the way through school believing that he's just made perfect report cards all the way, I would be fooling myself. Are we going to enter him in Harvard? Well, he hasn't got what it takes to go to Harvard and I let him go all this way without realizing it. I just don't think it tells me enough. Maybe, it even lets me be blind. Because it looks like he's doing terrifically. Great success all the way. When really he is doing all he can do but it isn't enough to expect Harvard or one of the better schools in the country to accept him."

Principal: "One of the things that we are working on is the parent-teacher conference. I think at the parent-teacher conference the teacher should be in a position to sit down with the parent and tell the parent specifically some of the areas of strength your boy has and some of the weak areas. Hopefully if that communication is open, then when you get the report card, you will have a better understanding of it. But I think you have pointed out a lot of concerns that we as school people have, as Miss R said; we have the problem of the child feeling repeatedly frustrated and having a lot of failure experiences which we don't want the child to go through. We know that the importance of the self-image is vital, especially in the elementary level, and if we don't give the child the confidence and the support he needs now, by the time he goes into junior high and high school, he will not be able to do as well as we would like him to. We want to balance this importance of self-confidence and self-image on the one hand with a realistic appraisal of the kinds of things he can do well and the areas he needs further help in. So I would say that the parent-teacher conference should be a vital part of this conferencing system and through this, the parent is informed better."

Mrs. C: "Yes, I agree. The last time I went for my second grader's evaluation, she's the one who seems to be doing quite well,

I sat down and her teacher said to me, 'Mrs. C, I have nothing to tell you; your daughter is just doing beautifully.' I was pleased to hear that. Any parent would be. But when I arrived home I looked at her report card. I realized that the teacher and I really chatted about irrelevant things. I had to look at her report card and then finally go back and ask the teacher as far as my daughter's reading was concerned, what the little symbol on the card meant. She told me, as a second grader, my daughter was reading in a third grade reader. This too is flattering but the teacher didn't even offer that information in the beginning. I had to go back and specifically ask, and I am confident there are parents who just don't ask. I think a teacher must be ready and willing to give out information. My children were going at that time to a nongraded school and the teacher told the P.T.A. what the nongraded school would be like. I asked that night, 'How will I know how my child compares?' Now I know it's a naughty word nowadays to compare children one with another, but still I like to know if my second grader is on a par with the rest of the second graders in the nation. Even if my daughter is low, I want to know that and the teacher said in order to know, you have to ask. Somehow that set very wrong with me. I don't think you should have to ask. I think you should be told."

Miss R: "Well, this brings up the standardized testing that's given in the third, fourth, fifth and sixth grades. But to give you an answer to your question, how will I know if my child is not Harvard material, actually, until he applies you will not know. It won't come from the report card and it never really did anyway."

Mrs. C: "Except, what do they base their applications on?"

Miss R: "Any number of things, not necessarily report cards."

Mrs. C: "If this reporting system went all through junior and senior high, how in the world would they ever choose a child for college? Certainly, not by ability, but by effort."

Miss R: "Well, you see we can get more information about effort from this kind of report card than from any other kind, but another question is what happens at the colleges. I think that's beginning to change also. It's very obvious that your standardized testing is where comparisons are made when it's important to make them; later on information on a child's school career as to how the child rates nationwide or how he stands in the total school community for children his age is received.

"But as far as the everyday progress made in a classroom and the year-to-year progress made in the elementary school, we feel strongly that children will do better when they begin to think about themselves as individuals. When they are confident enough and successful enough to be comfortable with education, with school, and with learning, then they will excel. We really believe this. Not every child is going to get into Harvard. We know this and children know this too, for built into this kind of a program is the thinking that you can do very much and you can do it well. One of the big things about a nongraded program is that children accept themselves as individuals and accept what they can and cannot do."

Mrs. C: "I agree with that philosophy wholeheartedly. I guess my main concern is not how you relate as a teacher and as an educator to my child but how you relate to me as a parent. I think I have a right to know what his level is! I like to know if he likes blue better than red. It's all part of knowing about my child."

Miss R: "Then I do think the thing that we should somehow have, whether it's on a report card or at a conference, is a way of telling parents a child's level; maybe not a number because that's an artificial designation but some way of saying your child is average, better than average, or a superior student. Now you see, if you had a child who received N's you would know more about your child than if he got S's."

Mrs. C: "That's true. I think this thing hit my husband and me the most; the one time that all three children came home and everything was S on the report cards. Then it occurred to us, 'What does this tell me anyway?' It told us that all three report cards were identical. You could have covered up the names and not have known the difference between them. Now that's disconcerting. It just didn't tell us enough. I keep saying that over and over because that was my feeling."

Miss R: "Well, it told you something; however, it wasn't what you were looking for. It did tell you that everyone of your children in the judgment of the teachers is performing at his or her expected level. Now, it does tell you that. It made no comparisons among your children. It didn't tell you which child is a better student."

Mrs. C: "No."

Miss R: "And this is the one thing we don't want to do."

Mrs. C: "Not to the child but to the parent."

Miss R: "This is something we don't want to do. No, even to parents. One of the hardest things teachers have had to learn to do is not to compare child A sitting next to child B and to say this one is a better student, he gets the ninety. I remember as a teacher saying, how do I know how to give ninety-three to one child and ninety-two to another? Give it to this one because he is a little bit better. I'll give him the ninety-three and him the ninety-two."

Mrs. C: "It wasn't based on percentages of material?"

Miss R: "Well, how carefully defined can it be for elementary school children? What is learning in elementary school? How accurate can you get? Why do you give this one an A and that one a B? This one is a little better, so he gets an A? A little better than what? And this is what you are trying to do with your children. Unconsciously because we grew up with this kind of thing, our background is such that when we say this one is a better student than the other, we really use a false standard. It's one we live with but it's false. It's not really necessary."

Mrs. C: "But even if that standard is on the basis of the judgment of the teachers, so is this."

Miss R: "Yes, but it's not based on a comparison with other children necessarily but based on what this child can do."

Mrs. C: "O.K."

Miss R: "Why is it now that your daughter who can read in second grade on the third grade level is doing that satisfactorily? She can be expected to do it. Maybe your fifth grader is reading on a fifth grade level. He cannot read on the sixth grade level yet. It would be unfair to make him read on the sixth grade level. He could not do that satisfactorily because it's not his level. But he is doing what he's capable of doing and he is doing it well. That is what's important."

Mrs. C: "I think that it is important and I do want to know that in junior high, where my older child is now, they tell me when he is working up to his ability in art. I want to know that."

Miss R: "No they don't. They give you an indication of effort. It's an effort mark."

Mrs. C: "Is that not synonymous?"

Miss R: "No. I don't think so."

Mrs. C: "If he puts in wholehearted effort, and he makes a one, which would indicate he is giving his best effort, would that not then be up to his ability?"

Miss R: "Well, what about the child who just cannot do it and he's working as hard as he can, or who can do a lot better and isn't putting any——"

Mrs. C: "Well, then his effort mark would coincide with his ability. Perhaps I have misconstrued it. Maybe, it's effort but still primarily it's the same thing."

Miss R: "You can make any scale work for you, you know, if you can think with it. You can interpret it so that it will work. It will give you an answer—something."

Mrs. C: "But it gives you not only that, but a mark as well. To me, it tells me more if he makes a one—which indicates supreme effort, than an eighty or a seventy. The report card would say to me, I don't have to put any kind of pressure on at home because at seventy in the teacher's eyes. . . ."

Miss R: "Suppose he got an N then? Not a seventy but an N. Wouldn't it tell you the same thing?"

Mrs. C: "It would tell me to put some pressure on. To try to work with him more at home, but it still wouldn't let me know what that level is. It wouldn't. I still like to know what it is."

Miss R: "I see. It's just that you know. If what you want to know is when your child needs more help from you or from the teacher, then when the card reads seventy or N, it says the same thing. The signal is the same."

Mrs. C: "Yes."

Miss R: "N means somewhere along the line this child needs help. He is not doing what you expect of him, and whether he gets a seventy, a sixty-five, an eighty or an N that signal is the same. Now if your child gets a one and eighty-five. . . ."

Mrs. C: "I'd say nothing as long as those ones are there."

Miss R: "Well, it's not the same as just getting an S."

Mrs. C: "Yes it is, as far as effort is concerned; it isn't as far as mental ability is concerned. I'd like to know."

Miss R: "But you can't do anything about that one and eighty-five."

Mrs. C: "I can't but I know it. I know."

Miss R: "I think again it is a frame of reference that we have developed in our own background and we have learned to think in terms of grades and it's a very difficult transition to another kind of thinking."

Mrs. C: "I am sure it is."

Miss R: "It has been very difficult for teachers to change this kind of thinking; to get away from a mind set that an eighty-five really means something very definite. Because of this problem, studies have been done with teacher's marks using the same papers, the same stories, or the same essay questions with different teachers marking them. Do you know that the grades given equalled A through D depending upon standards that each person sets? I am sure that the same thing is true for teachers who mark a set of papers in the classroom. When I know a child and I know that he really tries hard, I'll give him the extra five credits. I'll also mark a duplicate paper for another child saying he really wasn't putting all his effort into his work and I'll give a seventy-five. So marks can be very subjective."

Mrs. C: "I guess it's easier to relate to an A, B, C report card."

Miss R: "I think it's so because we've been used to a different kind of report card. But it really does not mean any more to a child or to us as parents when we think about it, for what we want to know about our children is are they working on a level at which they can be expected to perform?"

Mrs. C: "Then I must rely completely on the teacher to know what his expected level is?"

Miss R: "Yes, her decision comes from a judgment based on standardized tests as well as teacher judgment and experience. As your child gets older, expectancy will be based on the Iowa Tests, which are standardized and give nationwide scores."

Mrs. C: "Yes."

Miss R: "Teachers will also use the results of intelligence tests which give the teacher an indication of a child's natural ability. Teacher experience and observation are so very important. The teacher is still in some way saying, 'I know ten-year-olds should be able to do certain things. This is a ten-year-old with average ability who isn't doing these things. Then he is not working up to his level.' So it all comes into the picture. It's very difficult and you can't say it's only based on one thing."

Mrs. C: "No, and I understand the importance of not giving a child the feeling that he is superior or inferior because he is what he is. But I guess my whole feeling is that the parents should also be let in on how the school evaluates children."

Miss R: "I quite agree with that. I really agree that the parents should have a realistic understanding of their child and know whether the child is going to be Harvard material or whether the child should think about a vocation. Whether a child is going to be able to go to college or not, it's important for him to feel good about himself. The emphasis should not be such that if he can't get into Harvard, he isn't worth anything."

Mrs. C: "Yes, that's true."

Miss R: "You as an individual can become a marvelous plumber."

Mrs. C: "Sure."

Miss R: "I think one of the things you will find in the secondary schools is that when they give the children personality tests and occupational tests they do inform parents about the strengths of their child."

Mrs. C: "I am afraid sometimes we have become so individualized that we have forgotten what it is to live in a society. It even manifests itself in some of the riots we've had in the colleges. Some of the things these students are asking are non-negotiable. I want my way and that's all and it only points out again to me somehow that we have become too individualized. I, as a person, have become so important that it doesn't matter how I live in a community. I just don't want to get individualized to that point. I don't think we should have anything to do with it."

Principal: "I think what we are trying to do with children is to give them both group experiences and individual experiences and to build into each child an understanding of his responsibility as he works within the classroom with other children. When we talk about individualized instruction, we are talking about trying to meet the needs of the child on his level. So I would say that both the social experience of working with others and the experience of working at one's own level are both very important factors in a good school experience. I believe really what we are all saying is that a parent must become part of the evaluation system. Just as we know that a good teacher who sets a very fine relationship with the child has few problems and misunderstandings, so the teacher who has the ability to conference well with the parent is able to put across the concerns that she may have in working with the child. The kinds of questions that may go unanswered but are really there, are handled by a very astute teacher. I think we are talking about that.

"Well, thank you very much Mrs. C. We appreciate your coming and we hope that as we go on with our program, we will all better understand these involved areas of communication."

Mrs. C: "Thank you."

1. Did the teacher inform Mrs. C sufficiently about her daughter's work?
2. Do you think the supervisor answered Mrs. C to her satisfaction?
3. Is the satisfactory and the unsatisfactory report card better than the A, B, C card? What advantages and disadvantages does each system have?
4. Should parents be involved in developing a report card or should this be the jurisdiction of the school professional?
5. Do schools communicate well enough to parents so that parents know what the symbols on the report cards mean?
6. Do you agree with the principal that both social and individual experiences are the responsibilities of the school?
7. Do schools give children worthwhile social and individual experiences?
8. If the principal is correct when he states that the parent should be part of the reporting system then how should this be encouraged?

Mrs. C presents the concerns of many parents who do not understand the philosophy of the new report cards. They feel that the schools are not preparing children for life. As Mrs. C stated, "You should know where you stand from the beginning of life on through; then you are better equipped to handle it when you get into competing for jobs later in life."

Fathers, especially, will question the teacher about incentives and competition. Is the child getting lazy by simply receiving an S rather than a 79?

There is a great need to explain to parents that schools are not lowering their standards. Schools are realistic and expectations are held high. Competition is considered a part of everyday life. However, parents must be told that it is a matter of emphasis. The stress is placed on building a strong self-image based on success experiences in the elementary school.

Unfortunately, many teachers are not specific enough at a parent conference and they generalize about the progress of the child. Examples should always be cited showing concrete evidence of actually what the child is doing. Parents like to leave a conference with some very definite things to take home with them. Often a work paper or a creative piece of work may be given to the parent to take home.

The problem today is compounded by the fact that educators are more involved in the subtleties of education. The concern for the individualization of instruction, the emphasis on sound mental health practices in developing positive self-images, the search for more efficient learning techniques which involve student-learning styles and the development of student-teacher dialogues are all current practices which are both time consuming and require a greater amount of professional judgment than ever before.

Years ago parents were simply given a letter designation on their child's report card. This mark was accepted and not questioned. Today the teacher not only analyzes the child's class work but involves the parent in a dialogue on child growth and development.

CHAPTER NINETEEN

What Is a Parent

Supposed to Do?

This dialogue presents a concerned mother who has not been adequately informed about the school's program. To compound her confusion, her child has been transferred from a nongraded to a graded school and the mother is quite confused about grades and reading levels.

Unfortunately, the schools do not inform parents adequately about how the school functions. This mother is at a complete loss in trying to understand where her child is in reading.

Some schools have orientation programs for new parents at which time the principal talks about the kind of school organization and the kinds of facilities available for parents and children.

Some schools have class mothers who call new parents and help to answer some of their questions and to place the newcomer more at home.

In the case of the parent in this dialogue, the teacher should have made it a point to draw the parent out and to allay some of her fears. A direct presentation on the part of the child's teacher would have gone a long way to make the parent feel a little more comfortable about school.

Case no. 98M
Principal: "Good afternoon, Mrs. M. May I help you?"
Mrs. M: "Yes. I feel very badly about what I have to tell you,

but I believe this is a very important issue. As you know, my daughter is in the sixth grade at this school. I have a great deal of respect for you, your school, and your teachers, but we have a problem with released time."

Principal: "Oh!"

Mrs. M: "Yes. It seems that changing classes for math at the sixth grade is on Fridays, and strangely enough only on Fridays does it happen to come at the time when my child is supposed to be at released time. Now, she didn't tell me this for some time and then she became very upset. She was having tests on Friday. She missed the test and the teacher would give her the test on Monday and then she would miss the instruction on Monday. She's an average child. She does well enough in the average group, but this was quite a strain. I spoke to my child and I said, 'I can call the school. Perhaps they are not aware of this and there could have been a slipup,' but she was very hesitant about my doing it. However, week after week this went on. I called your supervisor. She was most sympathetic and said she was sure something could be arranged, and they did arrange with the teachers to change this math releveling to a time that was more appropriate. However, I think you should know that the supervisor mentioned to the teacher the parent who had made this request. A teacher mentioned it to my daughter in a nice way, saying, 'Well, I don't blame your mother for calling in. Of course, we didn't think we could change this for two or three people involved, but under the circumstance, yes, your mother was right.' Now everything was fine for a while until you had practice for graduation exercises, and one day when I appeared to pick up the children for released time, my daughter was missing. It seems that this time was part of their practice for graduation exercises and the teachers said she didn't have to be there. Well, how could she participate in this program if she didn't know the dance that she was supposed to do? So it was a conflict for my daughter and she chose to stay in school and be a part of her graduation exercise program. I feel that this is very sad for the child because she had to make a choice that I don't think the child should have to make."

Principal: "How many children are involved in this released time? Do you know?"

Mrs. M: "Very few children. There are only about three children who are involved in this program."

Principal: "I see. I wonder if the teacher really was aware due to the small number of children involved that this was actually happening? Did you have an opportunity to talk to the teacher about this before time?"

Mrs. M: "No, I never spoke to the classroom teacher because I found it to be a rather awkward situation. My daughter did not want me to interfere and I never spoke to the classroom teacher."

Principal: "Well, as I see it we wouldn't want to have a conflict between released time or religious training and other school time. Our approach has always been to permit the children, of course, to go to released time, and we have asked our teachers not to go into new work at that time but only to have review work. We would certainly honor your taking the child out to released time; I am wondering if maybe because you didn't see the teacher, she overlooked this and because there were only a few children, she didn't realize some were being called out at this point."

Mrs. M: "I would like to agree. She is a very understanding teacher, except at the beginning of the term when the class changed for math, the teacher was aware that this child was missing math. The child told the homeroom teacher she was and the teacher was quoted as saying, 'Well, we can't change the homeroom for three children.'"

Principal: "I see. Well I appreciate your coming to me and telling me about this because as I said before, we do want to avoid any problem where the child is put into a difficult position and must choose between going to religious instruction and staying at school. We will see that this doesn't happen again. I do appreciate your coming to tell about it. Is there anything else I could help you with?"

Mrs. M: "Yes, I have another problem. As you know, my youngster was in a nongraded school last year and on the report card, the teacher wrote that the youngster was reading very well. This was in first grade. Now I came to your school this year and your school is a graded school. The teacher told me the child is not reading well at all. Now I don't understand what this level four means, but I was told the child was fourth grade reading level last year. What is it about these schools? Don't they communicate to one another? What's the problem here?"

Principal: "Yes, they do communicate and sometimes when a child makes a change from one school to another, there is an adjustment period. Sometimes records do come in a little late, but generally this is not the problem. However, suppose I call Miss R in who is our supervisor and she can help us with this."

Mrs. M: "I'd appreciate that. Thank you."

Miss R: "Good afternoon, Mrs. M. How are you?"

Mrs. M: "Good afternoon, Miss R. Fine, thank you."

Principal: "A little problem here with a child coming from another school; a nongraded school to our graded one; possibly Mrs. M could just refresh us on this and I am sure we can help her."

Mrs. M: "Well, I am not saying what's wrong with your school, Miss R. My child was in a nongraded school last year and I have the report card here. It says my child does well and is on level four. I guess he is reading on fourth grade level. Now the teacher here tells me that this child is a very weak second grade reader; this comes as a great surprise and I am very upset. I don't understand. How come in one school a child reads nicely and in another reads below grade level?"

Miss R: "Well, Mrs. M, level four does not mean a fourth grade reader in the nongraded program. Level four is the fourth level of twenty levels and I am sorry that the teacher last year did not explain what that meant. I am sure your child was doing well at that level and was performing as well as he could be expected to perform. The nongraded philosophy may be a little bit different from our graded thinking and perhaps the teacher was not concerned or alarmed about the fact that the child was only level four at the end of the year. Was this at the end of the year?"

Mrs. M: "Yes, this was at the end of the first year."

Miss R: "Did you see your child's teacher this year?"

Mrs. M: "Yes, and I know that the child is now reading, but this was a shock. Why would the teacher on the report card say that the child was reading nicely when he was reading at the beginning of the first grade level at the end of the first grade? I don't understand that."

Miss R: "Well, as I said, I would imagine that this teacher was not thinking in terms of the child being a first grader or second grader but simply this was the level the child was performing on. The teacher felt that was all she could expect at that point and that he was performing at that level and doing well. He had reached that level at that point."

Mrs. M: "You're an educator and I am not, Miss R, and I don't understand what level four means and nobody told me. Now I have always heard grade level. No one ever told me level four was this kind of a thing. Somebody said my child was reading nicely; I think I was done some kind of disservice for no one told me exactly what that meant."

Miss R: "Did you attend any parent-orientation meetings on the nongraded program and on the reading program?"

Mrs. M: "I couldn't attend those. I know I was invited but I could not attend."

Miss R: "I am sure at those meetings you would have had the opportunity to understand how the reading levels were developed and what they meant and what four as opposed to grade four might mean. It is unfortunate you were unable to attend those meetings. I guess you didn't see the teacher either to learn just what level four meant, because you certainly have a right to know as a parent what that means. However, there is a little difference between grade level expectation and the individual child expectation when we measure a child according to grade level. Yes, level four for that matter would be the reading level, but if the teacher was satisfied that he was progressing and moving along and was doing nicely that would be what she was indicating to you."

Mrs. M: "Now Miss R, I can partly understand what you are saying, but what are you going to do for my child this year? What's going to happen at the end of second grade to my child? Is he going to be behind again? What do you think? I am very upset."

Miss R: "I would hate to think of or label your child as being behind. If your child has made a year's progress this year in his reading, then I would say he is doing very nicely."

Mrs. M: "Oh, now is this going to go on forever? He is going to be doing nicely but he is behind every year."

Miss R: "Perhaps, children do learn at different rates and have spurts and plateaus. We would have to determine his marks based upon his ability, his work habits and his skills, and there could come a time where he could accomplish what we might call his work in one year depending upon his growth rate."

Mrs. M: "I think my child is bright, but are you going to test him or something or what? How are you going to know?"

Miss R: "Yes, he should have had a California test this year and the result of that should be available for the teacher and should be available for you in the conference with the teacher. You should have some indication of your child's ability."

Mrs. M: "You are not going to keep my child back though. I know you are a graded school. Would you be keeping my child back this year?"

Miss R: "Not if we felt after a careful appraisal that retention would not help him. If this is his rate of learning and his rate of growth, I don't think we could say retention would do him much good and, therefore, we certainly would not. But there would be a very careful appraisal and evaluation by the teacher, myself and the principal before a decision such as that would be made."

Principal: "May I ask what the teacher said to you when you spoke to her about this year's work and also about your concern of a possible retention? Did the teacher speak to you about anything that would cause you alarm?"

Mrs. M: "No, but I'm just worried. I just didn't know my child was so low. I was under the impression my child was a good reader; my child is a very smart little boy and I cannot understand how he could be so far behind."

Principal: "Now the teacher did not give you any indication of the reason why she believed the child was behind?"

Mrs. M: "The teacher thought he was immature, but after all, last year's teacher did not say that and she thought he was doing very nicely. What is a parent supposed to think? This is what is really bothering me. There seems to be a communication problem some place here. Well, I didn't get to those meetings. Now part of that is my fault and maybe I just didn't understand how they evaluated children in that school, but I am concerned about my child this year in your school."

Miss R: "The evaluation is the same for both the graded and the nongraded school. We are still talking about children and what they accomplish and their expected level rather than about an artificial grade level, and certainly if your child at this point is working at his level and is doing what we can expect of him for now, there would be no real alarm or real concern. I would like to speak with the teacher. I would like to have an opportunity to get to know your child, observe him and to look through his records and see what more information I can glean before I make any other statement about him. But if I may, we can then set up a time where the three of us, the teacher, you and me, could sit down and discuss this and come to some very clear understanding so you will have a very definite picture of your son's ability and his accomplishments."

Principal: "What concerns me considerably is that here we are going on to the end of the year and this has just come to my attention. Now I was wondering if Miss R had heard about your concerns either through you or through the teacher. It seems to me if there is a concern, we want to know about it way before this. If there is a problem of communicating with the parent or if there is a problem in helping the parent and the child understand what the child's potential is, then it shouldn't wait until almost closing time."

Mrs. M: "Oh, I see. The child had a test. Was the teacher supposed to tell me what the child did on the California test you talked about?"

Principal: "When did we have a California test? Do you recall?"

Miss R: "In December, late December."

Mrs. M: "Now the teacher didn't tell me about that test."

Miss R: "When you had your second conference this year with the report card, I don't think the teacher told you about the test. But certainly in discussing the work your child was doing, the teacher told you the result of that test as a basis of her evaluation. Now, perhaps, her saying to you that he was reading below grade level and that she had some concern was the way she translated some data for you. Maybe the result of that test showed that your child has the ability to do better work and is not and maybe this is why she is concerned. Again, I would want to look into this more carefully. She has not consulted me about it and I do not know about this. Certainly there's been no talk of retention. As a matter of fact, we would have known by now."

Mrs. M: "I would appreciate that very much. I hope you understand my concern."

Miss R: "I certainly do and again I would want you to know that many children do catch up as they mature, especially little boys. Boys do make up for some of the time lost. They take a little longer in getting started, but I do think we ought to spend some time together in order to look at this more carefully."

Principal: "Do you think, Miss R, this may be the reason why the teacher wrote down on the card 'doing nicely'—in order to better understand the maturity level of the child and not to concern the parent? The teacher works with the child to bring him up to a level of performance that he may be able to handle. Do you think this is part of it?"

Miss R: "I think very often our first grade teachers do not have any objective evidence about children's ability. It's usually an intuitive thing and they are usually quite good about it. They also realize that little boys, especially, aren't always highly motivated to start reading at the very beginning of their school career anyway. Perhaps she felt she was getting very good things at the level at which he was working. He was doing well."

Mrs. M: "Yes."

Miss R: "And she did not feel at that point there was any reason for him to feel that he was a failure or to raise any concerns on your part."

Mrs. M: "Well, I am sure. She seemed very sweet and my child was happy last year, but I think she should have told me that, even though he was doing nicely, he really was quite far behind other children by the end of first grade. But I'd appreciate it if you would look into this."

Miss R: "Most certainly."

Principal: "We will have a conference on it. One thought that I have here. You feel your boy hasn't shown undue concern about his school work?"

Mrs. M: "No, no he seems quite happy."

Principal: "In other words, he is happy but you have the concern."

Mrs. M: "Yes."

Principal: "You have the concern. Well, as Miss R has said it may be the maturity factor, and if it is, it's a little different here; maybe the teachers have been trying to work with him to bring him along and yet not concern you. Generally, parents, and sometimes rightly so, get concerned with what children are learning and what they are not learning; yet if a child tends to be a little less mature than maybe some of the other boys around him, mother does build up these anxieties. Do you think this could possibly be part of it?"

Mrs. M: "I really feel better just having spoken to you people because I feel that you will give this a great deal of consideration and I think you are probably right. Maybe the teachers feel the child is doing the best that he can. He's simply immature. In other words, you are telling me not to worry. Isn't that what you're trying to say?"

Principal: "Yes. I would think so."

Mrs. M: "I should not be this concerned about my youngster."

Principal: "At this point I believe this is what we would say to you. I think Miss R would want to look into it further and will arrange for a three-way meeting with you and with the teacher so we can explore this further. But doesn't it appear to you, Miss R, mother may be just a little unduly concerned?"

Miss R: "This may very well be, and, as I said, I want to know more about this before I make any real judgment. Perhaps he's reaching a point now where we can begin to analyze why or what his weaknesses and his strengths might be in reading. We then can begin to work with those more intensely so he can come up to grade level in a short time."

Mrs. M: "Well, thank you very much. I don't want to take any more of your time and I'll be looking forward to hearing from you, Miss R."

Miss R: "It will be within a week or two, Mrs. M,—definitely."

Mrs. M: "Thank you."

1. Was the parent unduly concerned about her child's progress in reading?
2. Do you think the supervisor was talking over the mother's head?
3. How would you have approached this parent?
4. Do you think the principal was unduly concerned when he said, "What concerns me considerably is that here we are going on to the end of the year and this has just come to my attention"?
5. If you were the principal, would you have made that statement?

The immediate concern that Mrs. M brings to the school authorities is the conflict that occurred when the three students left for religious training and missed math instruction. This problem was compounded when Friday's released time was used as practice time for graduation exercises.

There is no question that the school was wrong in this case. New York state law is quite specific in stating that during released time review work should be planned.

Mrs. M is very concerned about having her boy transfer from a nongraded to a graded school. She is upset because the teacher in the nongraded school told her that he was doing nicely while at the graded school the teacher told her that her boy was a year behind.

Unfortunately, the supervisor talks to the mother about expected levels and reading abilities while all that the mother really needs is reassurance.

Sometimes school people do this with parents, and even when the schools provide orientation programs for parents, educators often talk on one level while parents grope for understanding on another.

The principal became a little upset when he realized that here was a mother whose questions had not been answered and the year was almost over.

The mother realized that her boy was immature, and when the supervisor talked about little boys taking a little longer, Mrs. M seemed almost relieved.

Here again a simple statement answers questions and confuses less than the educational jargon that this mother obviously did not understand.

CHAPTER TWENTY

After All That's

Said and Done

The compulsion to better know and help the hard-pressed teacher involved in the suburban school has led me to a better understanding of parent-teacher conference methods.

Nonconfrontational

The values of the nonconfrontational method seem peculiarly to fit the upward-mobile suburban parent. The parent due to his way of life is usually in a hurry, hard pressed and intense about what he is doing. This accelerated pace requires the parent to do many things in a short time. His scheduled day is so full that a limited amount of time must be allotted for each task and no more. As a result some parents overwhelm the schoolman, not usually because of hostility although there are some that do, but because time does not permit relationships to be developed gradually. They must concentrate their efforts and get to the point as soon as possible. This kind of approach may work in buying a piece of furniture, but it is hardly conducive to the developing of human relationships.

The nonconfrontational teacher understands this and he encourages the parent to talk out his concerns while structuring the conference to develop a positive relationship. He is sensitive to contemporary pressures and he is quick to evaluate the tone of the par-

204

ent so that he can better help him. He is sensitized to feel hidden hostilities toward school and he selects his words carefully when these feelings are evident.

The skills that the teacher and the administrator develop in accommodation are a result of the fact that the schoolman is servicing the public, but unlike the lawyer, he does not accept a fee from his client. He cannot refuse him his service. The parent is a taxpayer and through his elected board of education hires and fires the schoolman.

The schoolman therefore has developed ways of working with the public to insure his position as a public servant and also to try to further sound educational goals.

This public-servant concept has encouraged the teacher to develop skills in compromise, in arbitration and in viewing himself in a subordination-superordination relationship with the public. This relationship implies that one group, the public, has the upper hand while the professional educator is in a subordination position through a mutual understanding. Although this situation is changing through teacher militancy and in some communities personnel supply-and-demand problems, schools throughout the nation still have the background of the teacher as the subordinate in the relationship.

It is not by accident that teachers everywhere have developed skills in accommodating the public. Skills in developing an accepting atmosphere, avoiding conflict, listening to parent concerns, presenting positive information, correcting erroneous information and presenting factual data in a nonthreatening way are universally found among teachers as they work with hostile parents.

The upward-mobile suburbanite pressed for time, may frustrate the teacher-counselor in a first barrage of concerns. The teacher finds that by accommodating the parent these concerns may be dissipated and the teacher may be able to reassure the parent as he works with him.

The teacher may also be placed in a tense situation and precipitate a confrontation. This is not difficult because some parents accumulate a considerable amount of ammunition before going to a parent-teacher conference. When a parent tells the teacher that his private psychologist or pediatrician told him that the child is being improperly handled in school, this may lead to a coolness in the relationship.

The suburban schools have encouraged parents to participate on many levels in order to sell school bonds and budgets. Public support is curried and the P.T.A. president is actively involved in many supportive activities.

This type of encouragement produces a different kind of citizen. He is better informed and more involved than his city cousin in school affairs. He also has more of a say in what goes into the curriculum and what approach teachers use in working with children.

This change in approach from a "hands off policy" to "let's plan together" requires a skilled teacher who is well schooled in public relations and human dynamics. When parents are encouraged to discuss and to participate in school problems, the schoolman takes a calculated risk. He must be ready to accept an open situation and one that may not end as the schoolman planned.

The Teacher-Turned-Parent

One unusual aspect of this community participation in the schools is the difficult conferences that teachers sometimes have with fellow teachers whose children are in the school district.

Enough of these concerns have reached my desk to warrant a study. I have found that many teachers are able to switch hats when their turn comes to be the parent in a parent-teacher conference. There are other teachers though who have the utmost difficulty in changing roles.

I have grouped a number of characteristic symptoms of this occurrence which I call the hostile teacher-turned-parent syndrome. This condition is found in the teacher who views the parent's role as a passive one. He, as a teacher, does not accept the parent as one who should dialogue with him. He sees himself as an information-imparting teacher and he usually is quite vocal in the faculty room and at staff meetings. His arguments may be quite convincing and because he is forthright he has a following. This teacher has difficulty in changing hats in a parent-teacher conference. It would appear as though there is a clash in identity and a clouding of the roles played. He doesn't know how to "turn off" his role as a teacher.

Generally, the teacher has a highly structured ego and he may be known by his fellow staff members as a pile driver or as a go-getter. It is suspected that he may be using his parent identity as a way of lashing back at the teaching profession. He tends to be anxious and he verbalizes his concerns readily.

A nonconfrontational approach may or may not work for the teacher who is faced with this situation. Some teachers are quite successful in pulling the person up short and handling him most directly.

When a nonconfrontational approach is used the teacher-counselor would do well to allow the person to sound off and thereby ventilate his feelings. This outburst acts as a safety valve and may prevent a later explosion. The tense, anxious teacher readily explodes and this opportunity to complain may be all that is needed. An attempt should be made to suggest common ground so that as minor agreements are accepted the conference is restructured into a positive channel. This may be skillfully done by the teacher-counselor by emphasizing the shared professionalism of working with children. Obvious errors may be pointed out and agreed upon. This kind of approach gives the teacher-turned-parent a degree of satisfaction and it may open up other areas that can be agreed upon. The teacher leaves the door open for further discussion and invites the parent back again. Sometimes a note or a phone call will suffice. Here again the skillful teacher is able to pace himself and open only those areas that he thinks will be fruitful. He knows that working with a hostile teacher may involve so much time and energy that the little accomplished would hardly be worth the effort.

The hostile teacher-turned-parent shows up at board of education meetings, town planning meetings and at church organization meetings. Sometimes the chairman will give this individual a job to do either to shelve him or to channelize his energies into a positive area. However the person is handled, never lose track of the concerns that he has and remember that regardless of the approach used he should not go unnoticed.

The problem of the hostile teacher-turned-parent should be handled by the teacher's principal; however, a "live and let live" approach is often used where each professional draws a line over which the other is careful not to step. The principal shrugs his shoulders and says to himself that he has to accept certain things.

Unfortunately, such a teacher does monopolize staff meetings, tends to upset some of the already disturbed teachers on a staff and may encourage an already negative note in staff members who are easy to sway.

The principal has a responsibility to work with this person in whatever way he believes to be the most productive, for the teacher should not be permitted to run roughshod over fellow teachers, children and parents.

The School Triangle

The parent-teacher-principal triangle is another interesting aspect of the suburban parent conference. The principal is viewed by some parents as the one to turn to for instant satisfaction. This is often the case with the status-oriented parent who views the young teacher as immature and below the parent's station in life.

This parent views the school relationship in a similar way to the customer-saleslady-manager situation. If the customer does not get satisfaction from the saleslady he goes "to the top" and complains to the manager. A similarity exists when he goes to the superintendent or the president of the board to complain about the principal.

This going to the top man is also part of an accelerated way of life where time is limited and one goes directly to the decision-maker.

"The teacher can't help you, go to the principal, he makes the decision," is often heard.

Unfortunately, a teacher or a principal sometimes will tell a parent that this or that is not their decision and that it is out of their hands entirely. These kinds of comments further fortify a parent's belief that decisions are made at the top and the only way to get satisfaction is to go to the decision-maker.

Forward-looking schools counteract this approach by encouraging teachers and principals to make decisions on their level and to be responsible for carrying them out. This kind of approach encourages the school to act as a semi-autonomous unit where a high degree of professionism is developed.

Parents soon detect the kind of school system their children go to and they act accordingly. If they find that the president of the board can be encouraged to intercede in a parent-teacher concern, they will go to him. If on the other hand they sense that the teacher acts as a professional working within a team that is responsible for its own actions and decisions, then they act accordingly.

The parent conference is an art which requires many more skills and understandings than the schoolman has relegated to this area of home-school relationships.

The educator did not emphasize this activity in the past because the role of the parent was a rather cut-and-dried one. The parent viewed the schools as an imparter of knowledge and as a key to open doors of opportunity for his children. Many parents had less education than the schoolman and when a parent was called to school he viewed the schools as a symbol of authority.

The School as a Vehicle

Today the suburbanite sees the school as a vehicle that will help his child to learn marketable skills and develop the background needed in a upward-mobile society.

The parent may be more educated, better traveled and have had more success experiences than the teacher.

The suburban school is viewed less as a symbol of authority than as a tax supported service unit of the community.

The skilled suburban teacher is knowledgeable of these changes as he develops an awareness of the parent conference. He individualizes his approach knowing that each parent conference is unique.

This individualized approach to the conference implies that no one method can be mandated but the right approach to use will be based on the specifics of the case.

The teacher did well in the 524-A case to hear the parent out. An indirect approach worked. The principal utilized a nonconfrontational method with Mrs. J, case 628, and she left the conferences more secure about the school. Mrs. H, case 781, was given some guidelines with the direct approach while Mr. B, case 770, did not run roughshod over the teacher in a confrontational setting.

The teacher should be allotted a sufficient amount of time to research, prepare and administer a case conference. When this professional approach is used, the parent will have a better understanding of what the schools are all about and a closer alliance between parent and school will occur.

CHAPTER TWENTY-ONE

At the End

of the Rainbow

The school of the future will function as a social service complex completely integrated with local and state governmental organizations. There will be an exchange of skilled personnel and joint team planning so that the best minds of local, state and school people will work out common problems.

This will be a marked change for some communities because local governmental and school authorities jealously guard their own prerogatives. As a result there is a duplication of services, personnel and facilities that is wasteful. At a time when the education of the young is so vital to our existence and the pressures of an exploding population demand the best use of personnel and facilities we still have less than an intelligent sharing of our local resources.

The town planner will work closely with the school administrator and the school architect so that the suburban sprawl of today will be the planned building phase of tomorrow. Changes in zoning will be carefully weighed by local elected citizens and schoolmen.

The under-the-counter deal that is still too common between builder and town official is an anachronism which can no longer be permitted. The pressures of today's living and tomorrow's accelerated pace can no longer allow for any waste in the planning of community growth.

Racial integration will be perceived as a community commitment rather than as a political football or an idealist's dream. In-service work for both parent and teacher will ready a school for racial change. Needed dialogues between black and white teachers will precede bussing arrangements.

The pressures of population and the social changes of today will permit the integration of the schools of tomorrow. A change in the age of the population from an average of twenty-five today to one even younger tomorrow will further encourage social change.

Boards of education, administrations and school staffs will have many black people rather than the token sprinkling of middle-class blacks we have today.

A Community of Purpose

The schools will work closely with the civic, fraternal and religious groups in the community so that there will be a community of purpose, namely, helping children grow and develop.

There will be fewer misunderstandings among the different power groups in the community because communications will be developed based upon the benefits that will accrue from helping one another.

There will always be opportunists and neurotics who will stir up trouble; however, with a clarification of community goals and the pinpointing of responsibilties these dissident voices will be less effective.

Rapprochement between the parochial and public schools so long needed and yet tacitly ignored will occur based upon cooperation and dialogue. An understanding that all children become citizens regardless of schooling will be a reality. No longer will some children sit in parochial classrooms with forty-five other children and share textbooks, circa 1940.

The fears of yesterday's church-state conflicts will be dissipated as communities begin to place emphasis where it really belongs, on the need for all citizens of the community to be involved in total participation. Decision-making problems in local government rather than outworn concerns about church-state differences will be paramount.

The school will contain a mental-health clinic wing which will be administered by the town government with representatives on its governing body from the schools and from the various local religious groups. The facilities of this unit will share personnel with the schools so that waiting lists for psychological, social-work and counseling services will be minimized.

The sharing of these facilities and responsibilites by government, school and religious groups will encourage a working together that has only been touched upon.

The need for the clergy and the schoolman to work together in servicing children and parents has been all but overlooked. The fear of each group transgressing on the other one's territory has lessened the effectiveness of both the clergyman and the schoolman.

The school will be able not only to refer children to the clinic but also teachers, administrators and parents. The need to render valuable psychological guidance services to people today is hampered by permission from the family. This will no longer be the case as the citizen begins to realize the human waste involved.

Rather than wait, as is done today, for the adult to ask for help for himself or for the family to give permission for its child to be helped, the determination of whether or not to give psychological help will be based on objective tests.

The emphasis upon the uniqueness of each child will encourage the schools to view child development no longer as an academic enterprise but as a total commitment to individual development. The teacher will encourage verbal and written expression through a multiplicity of media. Exposures of various sorts will permit the child to work with teams of teachers, parents and children.

The concept of one teacher in a self-contained or a semi-self-contained classroom will no longer be acceptable. Classroom walls will be nonexistent and the use of teacher-specialists and para-professionals will be widespread.

The key educator will still be the teacher but his role will be one of a catalyst. The primary child will no longer waste time in a grade he has already outgrown or is not prepared for but will be placed in a section that best fits his needs. As he progresses into the intermediate levels he will have more freedom to take advantage of the various learning centers of the school.

The Educational Complex

The school will view the parent as an integral part of an educational complex. The responsibilities of the parent will be more involved and time-consuming than in today's school. The parent will receive an initial orientation program in school philosophy and procedure when entering the school community. He then will have an opportunity to attend seminars with teachers and other parents to become more aware of existing school problems and changes in curriculum.

The trend of giving the school more and more responsibility for the child's total welfare to the point where some teachers have said, "Someday we instead of the parents will have responsibility for the children even while they are babies," will be changed.

The parent will be more involved in the school as a responsible team member with teachers and other community leaders. The parent will work with others to develop solutions for shared problems.

The responsibility for the moral development of the child will be placed where it belongs, with the parent. This first line of instruction will then be supported by the clergy and the schools.

The parent will continue to be involved in utilizing the school facilities, only now the facilities will be open to the public seven nights a week, twelve months a year.

The need to further develop a parent commitment in support of the schools will be stressed by the community through its parent-teacher organizations. The state and national governments will have taken over much of the financial commitments of the school so that the local parent-teacher associations will be able to utilize their energy in helping to improve the parent's perception of the school rather than spending it on concerns over budgets, bond isues and buying audio-visual aids.

Special parent-teacher meetings to encourage the parent to think about the involvement he has in child rearing, in developing sound school attitudes and in working in a positive way with teachers all will be included in a program aimed at developing an aware parent.

The parent will be part of evaluation teams not only to review the curriculum and its implications but also to review parent-teacher conference outcomes so that the best ideas of the school community may be harnessed to good advantage.

This approach assumes that the educational leaders—the teachers, principals and superintendents—will be truly secure in their roles and able to maintain themselves as professional educators.

Many educators shy away from parent involvement in curriculum development and in sharing educational problems with parents. The confusion here is one of differentiating the role of the professional who is an expert in his field and the supportive role of the parent who is a partner in the educational enterprise.

Coffee klatches, housing development meetings and apartment house get-togethers will supersede the supermarket and the beauty parlor chit-chats as information centers.

There will still be parents who will be dissatisfied with the schools and with particular teachers. However, all parents will have an opportunity to participate actively in school affairs and every citizen will be well informed about curriculum change and school procedures.

The parent conference will have taken the place of the written report card so that the parent and the teacher through face-to-face contacts will be better able to understand each other and in turn help the child.

Teacher education will have undergone a definite change. The interne-teacher program will be a common pratice. The fifth-year program which includes a master's degree will encompass part-time teacher placement in the schools on a paying basis. Joint evaluations by the local school people and the college advisor will be an in-depth interaction that will require the master teacher to take time off from his class to work at the college with the interne teacher's advisor. Opportunities for the interne teacher to experience a variety of parent-conference situations will be realized. A course in parent-conference methods will be required.

Teacher Training: A Sixth-Year Experience

A sixth-year program will be the equivalent of the first full-time paying position of the teacher as a member of a local school staff. The teacher may or may not be responsible for a class of children.

He may be involved in a team operation where he will assume certain teaching responsibilities during the day. He may work with several master teachers as he aids in classroom teaching activities. Part of each school day will be used in working with the principal, supervisory personnel and, depending on the size of the educational enterprise, the college clinician and advisors whom the college can make available. Work in the mental health clinic and the school district's reading and learning centers will prepare him for a truly professional career. The state government will help to defray the expenses of the sixth-year experience.

It is expected that by the time the teacher has completed his sixth-year experience he will have developed an awareness of human relationships as well as skills in teaching the academic areas.

The security-building relationships that the neophyte teacher has so far been involved in will give him a commitment to parent-conference approaches and parent-involvement activities. He will then be able to work in a truly professional setting without too many qualms about his relative lack of experience.

The colleges will also have had an opportunity to screen their students as to whether they are psychologically able to work with other people. No longer will students go into education because they think it is an easy way out.

Unfortunately, many students still believe that if they can't get into engineering or medical school they can go through a series of "Mickey Mouse courses" and get a degree and teach.

Some women students are counseled by their mothers to get a teacher's certificate, teacher a bit and then when the children arrive, leave teaching only to go back later. The mother sees this as security for her daughter and a way that her daughter may help her husband get on his feet.

The local school and the college clinician through constant meetings will be better able to evaluate the ability and the soundness of the neophyte.

The Principal of the Future

The principal of the future will be the educational catalyst of the local school enterprise. He will no longer be seen as the final word in the teaching and the management of all school areas. His role will be that of an educational innovator, a prime mover in activating community support and as a chairman in working with various teacher, parent and student action groups.

This change in role will necessitate a different orientation and training for the principal. He will have to be not only more sensitive to people but more skilled as a community worker.

No longer will seething resentments on the part of parent or teacher go unnoticed until they reach a boiling point. The principal will be aware of changing times and concerns, and will help to restructure feelings into positive channels so that change may be brought about in an efficient manner.

As the interpreter of change in his local school he will be able to relate to the larger school organization and bring to bear his insights and understanding. He and other administrators in the school district will act as pace-setters so that the teachers will see them as instruments of their professional concerns. He will work closely with his professional staff so that changes and recommendations for changes will be the result of the staff's thinking and acting together rather than of a single person's decisions.

The principal will be greatly involved with the parent as he works with a more aware and a better informed citizen. His role as the third man, the balance wheel in difficult parent-teacher relationships, will be more needed. His judgment in evaluating parent and teacher concerns will be emphasized. The greater acceleration of the community's pace and the further explosion of knowledge will require that he become increasingly sensitive to people's feelings.

The Role of the Student

The elementary student will be involved in the understanding and the absorption of greater amounts of knowledge than ever before. He will have at his disposal newer and more efficient audio-visual aids, learning devises and special personnel.

The student will have greater freedom in choosing different areas and ways to study than ever before.

This freedom will require more responsibility on his part. He will have to discipline himself to better utilize his time and talents as he moves about the building and the community to seek out resource materials.

The student will have opportunities to discuss with teachers and with fellow students the values of education. He will be more aware of the contribution of the public school to his growth and development.

The trend to have pre-reporting conferences between student and teacher will be accelerated so that the student will be very aware of any reports that are later discussed between the parent and the teacher.

The values of the parent-teacher conference will be better understood and the child, when he sits at the dinner table, will interpret things that are going on in school in an intelligent way, which is often not the case today. Witness the father who asks his son what happened in school today and the boy answers, "nothing."

The board of education may still be elected by the public, but it will be less of a popularity contest or "vote for me, I've got a gripe" situation. There will be a greater representation of the different community interests and levels.

The board member will not usurp the superintendent's prerogative as administrator of the schools or dictate what should or should not be taught. The board member will aid the community and the professional teaching staff by facilitating good education. He will do this by developing school policy that is supportive of the way an enlightened public and a forward-looking professional staff want to go.

Parents will still reach some board members about teacher-parent conflicts that should be settled on a local level. Misunderstandings will still reach his ears about the administrator. However, through state workshops for board members he will be better able to perceive his role and leave parent concerns to be handled by the building principals.

Do some of these projections appear visionary? I hardly think so. Some schools have started to experiment with buildings that have no inner walls so that they may break away from the concept of having one adult in a box with thirty children. Some principals are perceiving their roles more as advisors and initiators of change than as the traditional head teacher.

Some schools have developed highly sophisticated parent-teacher conference methods.

The seeds of change are already planted in a democratic setting where the forward movement of a young action-centered public demands new and better ways of educating the young and of relating to each other.

Glossary of Terms

Accommodation—A way by which groups and/or individuals may work cooperatively, even if on a limited basis.

Adult-centered society—A community whose goods and services place an emphasis on the adult population.

Arbitration—A form of accommodation where a third party is brought in to settle a dispute.

Child-centered society—A community whose goods and services place an emphasis on the child population.

Compromise—Agreement to give way but still maintain a position.

Confrontation—A hostile meeting of people which is highly charged.

Dialogue—Verbal interaction between two individuals or among groups of people in order to develop further understandings.

Hostile teacher-turned-parent syndrome—A series of characteristics found in the disgruntled teacher who when interacting with the schools as a parent finds it difficult to assume the parent role.

Mickey Mouse courses—The term that teachers and students of education use in referring to education courses. In using this term, teachers and students are poking fun at college courses which are repetitive and embellished to the point where they are considered comical.

Nonconfrontational method—A structured approach in working with an individual so that hostility is dissipated and a positive relationship and understanding is developed.

Parent-teacher-principal triangle—A relationship based upon the assumption that the parent can go directly to the principal for satisfaction.

Self-contained classroom—An organizational pattern where the classroom teacher instructs the children in all subjects.

Semi-autonomous unit—An organization that is able to make decisions on the local level and that relates to a central organization through representation.

Semi-self-contained classroom—An organizational pattern where the classroom teacher instructs the children in most subjects. Generally, special teachers instruct the children in art, music and physical education.

Status-oriented parent—The parent who measures himself and others by the socio-economic position of the individual.

Subordination–superordination relationship—One group has the upper hand through a mutual understanding.

Suburban sprawl—The tendency for growth patterns in suburban housing areas to spread out.

Teacher-counselor—The educator who participates in a one-to-one relationship with a parent with the express purpose of giving guidance.

Upward-mobile suburbanite—The suburbanite who is actively striving to better his social and economic position.

Bibliography

Bailard, Virginia, and Ruth Strang, *Parent-Teacher Conferences.* New York: McGraw-Hill Book Co., Inc., 1946, 216 pp.

Board of Education—City of New York, *Guidance of Children in the Elementary Schools.* July, 1960.

Bullis, H. Edmund, and Emily E. O'Malley, *Human Relations in the Classroom.* Wilmington, Delaware: State Society for Mental Hygiene, 1947.

Detjen, Ervin W., and Mary F., *Elementary School Guidance.* New York: McGraw-Hill Book Co., Inc., 1963.

D'Evelyn, Katherine, *Individual Parent-Teacher Conferences.* New York: Bureau of Publications, Teachers College, Columbia University, 1945.

Gesell, Arnold, and Frances L. Ilg, *The Child From Five to Ten.* New York: Harper and Row, Publishers, 1946.

Gruenberg, Sidonie Matsner, *The Parents' Guide to Everyday Problems of Boys and Girls.* New York: Random House, Inc., 1958.

Heffernan, Helen, and Vivian Todd, *Elementary Teacher's Guide to Working With Parents.* West Nyack, N.Y.: Parker Publishing Co., Inc., 1969.

Hymes, James L., Jr., *A Pound of Prevention*. New York: Teachers Service Committee on the Emotional Needs of Children, 1947.

———. *Behavior and Misbehavior*. Englewood Cliffs, N.J.: Prentice-Hall, Inc., 1955.

———. *Being a Good Parent*. New York: Bureau of Publications, Teachers College, Columbia University, 1949.

———. *Effective Home-School Relations*. Englewood Cliffs, N.J.: Prentice-Hall, Inc., 1953, 264 pp.

Jenkins, Gladys Gardner, Helen Schacter, and William W. Bauer, *These Are Your Children*. Chicago: Scott, Foresman and Company, 1953.

Kowitz, Gerald T. and Norma G., *Guidance in the Elementary Classroom*. New York: McGraw-Hill Book Company, Inc. 1959.

Lane, Howard, and Mary Beauchamp, *Human Relations in Teaching*. Englewood Cliffs, N.J.: Prentice-Hall, Inc., 1955.

Langdon, Grace, and Iriving W. Stout, *Helping Parents Understand Their Child's School: A Handbook for Teachers*. Englewood Cliffs, N.J.: Prentice-Hall, Inc., 1957.

Leonard, Edith M., Dorothy D. Vandeman, and Lillian E. Miles, *Counseling With Parents in Early Childhood Education*. New York: The Macmillan Co., 1954.

Piers, Moria, *How to Work With Parents*. Chicago: Science Research Associates, 1955.

Rogers, Dorothy, *Mental Hygiene in Elemetary Education*. Boston: Houghton Mifflin Co., 1957.

Schenectady Public Schools, *Parent Teacher Conference Guide*. Schenectady, N.Y., 1964.

Stout, Irving, and Grace Langdon, *Parent-Teacher Relationships*. Dept. of Classroom Teachers Am. Ltd., Research Assn. of the N.S.A., 1958.

Symonds, Percival M., *The Dynamics of Parent-Child Relationships*. New York: Bureau of Publications, Teachers College, Columbia University, 1949.

APPENDIX A

Preplanning Techniques in the Conference

Arrange for the conference to be held in a quiet place. Adult-size chairs should be used away from the teacher's desk.

Schedule the conference time so that no participants are rushed.

Create a relaxed atmosphere where mutual fears may be dissipated.

Assemble a file of pertinent samples of the student's work.

Review the anecdotal record for significant data.

Evaluate recent test results in the light of pupil's performance.

Contact other teachers for their observations and insights concerning the student.

Consider the value of interviewing the pupil before the conference.

APPENDIX B

Useful Hints in the Parent Conference

Begin the conference on a positive note.

Present some of the student's accomplishments.

Attempt to understand the parent's feeling.

Maintain a professional attitude throughout the conference.

Allow the parent to talk out his concerns.

Help the parent to find his own solution to the problem when possible.

Avoid pedaguese. Explain new concepts and terminology in a simple manner.

Do not take notes during the conference.

Write out conference comments immediately after the parent leaves.

Refrain from giving advice on personal and family problems.

Structure the conference so that the reason for the meeting may be realized.

Conclude the conference on a positive note.

APPENDIX C

The Parent-Teacher Conference Form may be used by the class-room teacher as he completes the parent conference. This form may be placed in the student's permanent record folder for future reference.

Parent-Teacher Conference Form

Name of Parent _____ Name of Teacher _____

Name of Child _____ Date of conference _____

BASIS OF DISCUSSION:

CLIMATE OF THE CONFERENCE:

OUTCOME OF THE CONFERENCE:

The Parent-Teacher Conference Form Card may be used by the teacher and/or the principal as a ready reference on the conference. This 5″ x 8″ card may be easily filed.

Front of card

Parent-Teacher Conference Form
Name of Parent:
Name of child:
Name of teacher:
Date of conference:
Basis of discussion:

Back of card

Climate of the conference:
Outcome of the conference:

The Parent-Teacher Conference Worksheet Form may be used to study parent conferences. This form allows for a comparison of different conference approaches.

	PARENT-TEACHER CONFERENCE WORKSHEET			
	Approach	*Basis of Discussion*	*Climate of the Conference*	*Outcome of the Conference*

This sheet is made available to the parent prior to the conference. It is filled out and sent to the teacher before the conference.

Parent-Conference Preplanning Sheet

Child's name _____

Parent's name _____

Date and Time of Conference_____

I am specifically interested in finding out about the following areas and concerns at the time of our conference:

I do appreciate your help in giving me information on these matters.

Parent's signature _____

The Follow-Up Conference Information sheet enables the professional involved in a parent conference to gather additional information from fellow professionals.

Follow-Up Conference Information:

I have had a conference with _____ regarding

_____

Kindly list any information that you have that may prove helpful.

Requesting professional's name _____
date _____

Sending professional's name _____
date _____

The Parent-Conference Questionnaire gives the parent an opportunity to state his reaction to the conference and it enables the teacher to gather information about the conference.

Parent-Conference Questionnaire

Dear Parent,

Kindly fill out this form after your conference.

Your reactions will be most helpful to us in evaluating this conference.

I found this conference worthwhile because

_____
_____
_____
_____
_____

This conference could have been improved by

_____
_____
_____
_____
_____

It is not necessary to sign this form.

The Intensive-Conference Form may be used by the teacher and/ or the principal when an in-depth study of a parent conference is warranted.

Intensive Conference Form

Name of Parent: _____
Name of Child: _____
Name of Teacher: _____
Date of Conference: _____

Reason for Conference:

Teacher-Parent Conference Notes:

Teacher-Special-Area Personnel Notes:

Teacher-Student Conference Talk:

Anecdotal Behavioral Notes:

(*over*)

Special Classroom Observations by Other Professionals:

Test Results:

Tentative Conclusions:

Index

V

Visits (*see* Home visits)
Vocational training, 52

W

Worksheets, 92
Workshops, for board members, 217
Work-study habits, 57, 59-60, 71